GETTING PAST PERFECT

HOW TO FIND JOY AND GRACE IN THE MESSINESS OF MOTHERHOOD

GETTING PAST PERFECT

HOW TO FIND JOY AND GRACE IN THE MESSINESS OF MOTHERHOOD

KATE WICKER

Foreword by **Rachel Balducci**
Afterword by **Lisa M. Hendey**

Ave Maria Press AVE Notre Dame, Indiana

Founded in 1865, Ave Maria Press is a ministry of the United States Province of Holy Cross.

www.avemariapress.com

Paperback: ISBN-13 978-1-59471-716-1

E-book: ISBN-13 978-1-59471-717-8

Cover image © iStockphoto.

Cover and text design by Katherine J. Ross.

Printed and bound in the United States of America.

Library of Congress Cataloging-in-Publication Data is available.

To my children:
Madeline, Rachel, M. E., Thomas, and Baby No. 5. Thank
you for the privilege of being your mama and for loving and
accepting imperfect me. I love each of you just the way you
are, and I thank God for each of you every day.

For my own mom: I learned from the very best. I love you
more. (Top that!)

She could never be a saint, but she thought she could be a martyr if they killed her quick.

—"A Temple of the Holy Ghost," Flannery O'Connor

Contents

Foreword

BY RACHEL SWENSON BALDUCCI

Motherhood is not for wimps.

I say this often.

I say it when I give talks to groups of women who need encouragement. I say it in conversations with friends as we pour out our hearts in frustration or fatigue. I say it to myself when the trenches I'm in feel a little deeper than I'd like.

Motherhood, my dear, sweet child of God, is not for wimps.

Being a mom is the hardest thing you will ever do and one of the most important. And that's why, if we start thinking about things too much, we can get a little carried away. I want to do the absolute best job I can at being a mother to my children. God gifted these children to me! My husband and I cocreated these souls with the King of the universe! If I fail at motherhood, I feel like I've failed at life!

You can see why things can get a little intense. There is so much riding on our job. If we fail, if our children don't turn out perfectly, then the fate of the free world will crumble and fall.

But it won't. I hope you recognize how ridiculous that sounds.

We've all been there, too much in our own heads, taking ourselves and our jobs as mothers just a little too seriously. We need to be serious about it, of course, but if we get too caught up in all of this relying on us and our own amazing capabilities, we will send ourselves spiraling into failure.

Because no one is perfect. That's the sad, beautiful reality of life. We need to get past perfect and get into the loving arms of Jesus.

We want to be perfect—but perfect in the the Lord.

We want to be the best—by using the tools God has given us.

We want to do right by our children—but in the eyes of God, and not the world.

I'm excited about Kate's book, about the reminder that we need to stop focusing on being perfect and start being real. The reality of raising our children to know, love, and serve Jesus (our goal as parents) is that we operate out of a real sense of God's great love for our children—and for us. Jesus loves me so much that he will give me every good thing to help guide my children to the way of peace.

Thank you, Kate, for this book that reminds us that each one of us is called to be the best mom we can be, embracing our imperfections along the way. It's all about trust in Christ. And once we accept the reality that we aren't perfect (and talk about it openly), then we can start being the kind of mothers Jesus wants us to be.

There is freedom in getting past perfect. Because once we stop trying to be the best at *all the things*, we can put God in control and rely on his loving hand to guide us in this beautiful vocation.

Motherhood isn't for wimps. But it is for real women—just like you and me, who are learning to say, "I'm not perfect, but I'm perfect in Christ."

Introduction

FEAR IN MOTHERING

In the midst of an evening storm last summer, a jolt of jagged lightning cut through the darkness, cutting off our electricity. So the kids and I gathered together in my bedroom and read by candlelight. They cuddled close and listened to books filled with beautiful imagery. We weren't doing anything grand, but no one was fighting, and everyone seemed content. It felt like we were exactly where we were supposed to be—together and safe from the storm churning outside.

Oftentimes, the storm isn't outside of our home; it's right in the middle of it, and no one is safe from the whirlwind of mess, heightened emotions, and chaos that seems to follow us everywhere we go.

Just recently, we were rushing out the door, and my kids were dawdling, fighting, singing loudly, leaving a trail of detritus, telling me exceedingly long stories, and getting angry because I wasn't making constant eye contact with them. Basically, they were driving me absolutely nuts.

My inner White Rabbit was unleashed, and I was repeatedly hollering, "We're late! We're late! We're late!"

Our tardiness didn't seem to bother the kids at all; they continued to move in slow motion except when they were lashing out at a sibling. Then their arms were windmills of thrashing motion.

But I was not ready to surrender. I dug in my heels more deeply and barked my orders more loudly. Like a raging tsunami—what my oldest and I joke is my alter ego, the tsu-mommy—I stormed through the house.

This is exactly the kind of mom I don't want my children to remember. I want them to just think of my face, calm and serene in the candlelight, reading books while I shielded them from the summer storm—instead of allowing us to become part of one.

After yet another failed search-and-rescue mission for MIA shoes, I corralled the kids into my car. During the entire ride, I lectured, nagged, and droned on and on, but none of this made me feel any better. Nor did any of my didactic diatribes seem to sink in with my children. I am disappointed to announce that at the time of this book's publication, they continue to misplace shoes, so much so that I'm starting to suspect our home is the Bermuda Triangle for footwear. In all likelihood, all my children probably heard in my chiding was "Wah-wah-wah," as if I were an adult in a *Peanuts* show.

When I dropped the kids off at school, there was a flurry of rushed "good-byes" and "I love yous." As soon as the van doors slid shut, I was left alone with my fears and insecurities, and a tangle of questions dashed across my mind: *Why am I not a more patient mother? A more joyful mother? Why don't my children ever seem to respond to empathetic limits—or my drill sergeant orders? Why do I have to remind my children millions of times to put their shoes back in the proper place or to do this or that yet they still keep managing to forget? Why do I so frequently feel like an epic failure when it comes to being a mom? Why do these lovely children of mine sometimes drive me absolutely crazy? What is wrong with me?*

I know I'm not the only mother who asks questions like these. While most moms have a decent archive of happy moments with their children as well as occasions when they feel like they got it right as mothers, the fear of failure weighs heavily on most of our mothering shoulders.

Motherhood is tough, and guilt that we're not doing this mothering gig properly seems to be woven into our DNA. Yet so many of us are afraid to reveal our fears, our struggles, or the fact that as much as we love our children, they do sometimes feel like a burden. Because if we acknowledge those awful truths—that we sometimes feel overwhelmed or discontented, that mothering isn't always a source of bliss or fulfillment—then what does that say about us as mothers and, even more so, as Christians?

—

When I was a few weeks from submitting this very manuscript, I discovered I was pregnant with my fifth child. For the first time in my mothering journey, seeing those two little lines appear did not evoke feelings of excitement or happiness. Instead, I was scared, frustrated, and sad. What's more, because I felt all of those less-than-desirable emotions when I thought that I *should* be feeling blessed and excited, I experienced powerful waves of guilt. *If I believed children were gifts from God, how could I be feeling so resentful?* Instead of reflecting upon how this baby would enrich my life and my family, all I could focus on was how a new child would complicate an already overwhelming, over-leveraged, and overextended life. I also selfishly kept thinking about how I'd *finally* started having a little more alone time that didn't require me setting an alarm clock for 4:30 a.m.

All of these feelings were normal for a mom who, only a few months prior, had accepted the size of her family; decided to remove all traces of all things "baby" and gave *everything* (everything!) away; and was really starting to appreciate this new season of her life and not having any bums to wipe on the hour. God has a hilarious sense of humor. Just *hilarious*.

I don't often admit or say aloud the bleak kinds of thoughts I had after I discovered I was pregnant as well as the anxious questions I ask myself whenever I have a bad day.

In Christian circles—where we're fervently fighting against a culture that too often devalues children and motherhood—it can be scary and feel unsettling to speak the truth and share any of our more negative feelings and experiences as parents.

But when we sugarcoat motherhood and fail to be authentic mothers, we actually do our families a disservice. By hiding behind "everything is wonderful" or, at the very least, "I'm fine" masks, we dismiss the cost of motherhood. And there *is* a cost. If motherhood is a path to sanctity, then we ought to expect some bumps along the road. As Mother Angelica said, "Holiness is not for wimps and the cross is not negotiable, sweetheart, it's a requirement."[1]

As Christians, we have to be careful to not simply bask in the glory of Jesus' birth and Resurrection while completely glossing over or ignoring the Passion. We can't appreciate the sacrifice of the Cross or the need for a Savior if we don't recognize and regard Jesus' suffering and death and our own brokenness.

This was depicted poignantly on the cover of a 2013 issue of *Time* magazine that featured a picture of a beautiful couple with toned bodies and blissful smiles sunbathing under the headline "The Childfree Life." As someone who works in media, I immediately recognized the cover had its own sensationalist agenda. Honestly, the toothy couple reminded me more of advertising than journalism. Showing a good-looking, childless couple was a savvy marketing campaign that delivered a message like this: *Forgo pregnancy, adoption, or any other way of acquiring soul-sucking money pits, also known as children, and you, too, can travel the world, find the ultimate kind of happiness, and look like a movie star.*

The cover definitely suggested that choosing not to have children can be equated with greater happiness or, at the very least, with more freedom to pursue things that might make you happy. On the flip side, I believe the Christian parenting camp has been guilty of using its own alluring marketing: *Children are always blessings, not burdens! You don't know what real happiness is until you bring a child into the world. They're hard work, but they're worth it. They give far more than they take! Having children is the "be all and end all" to living a happy, fulfilling life!*

We also have the tendency to see those who don't have children—or perhaps openly admit how hard it is to parent them—as more selfish. Although the primacy of self may be partly to blame for people choosing the childless life, it could be argued that it's sometimes to blame for choosing to have kids, too. We want the good without the bad. We want the cuddles and kisses without the poop, tantrums, or defiant toddlers and tweens. We want the teenagers sans the hormones. We want to kiss a boo-boo and immediately see all the pain washed away. We don't want to hurt or see our kids hurt. We certainly don't want to hurt our own kids. We invest in our children because that's what parents do but also because we expect a return for our investment. We want to see the fruit of our work ripen well and become something beautiful. We want to bring virtuous and content people into the world; we don't want to create slaves to addiction or depression or worldly desires as sons or daughters. But becoming a parent forces us to face *and* admit our fears. It's not about us or our desires. It's not even about our happiness. Motherhood, like nothing else in my life, has forced me to relinquish control, to trust, and to look beyond myself as well as my own limitations.

We all have fears and struggles as moms, and it's time we start sharing them. In doing so, we're able to free ourselves from some of the worry that we're the *only* ones who have "difficult" children who push our buttons and yes, at times annoy us. When we admit that being a mom is the hardest job we will ever love, we're giving others permission to be authentic as well and to share their own private doubts about their maternal competency. When we share in the mess of maternity and humanity, we're telling the secular world that might question the value of children and motherhood that it's a difficult thing but the fact that we're acknowledging the struggle yet still waking up each day shows that it's worth it.

As author and speaker Brené Brown writes, "The dark does not destroy the light; it defines it. It's our *fear of the dark* that casts our joy into the shadows."[2]

Are you ready to embrace the darkness—the not-so-nice aspects of motherhood—in order to better appreciate the light? Are you ready to admit that yes, you sometimes yell at your children but you love them so very much and want to try harder not to? Do you want to be a more joyful mother but find yourself feeling like an empty shell of a person with a slapped-on smiley face? Are you prepared to unload the guilt that burdens you, not by trying to do *more* as a mother but simply by trusting in God, his providence, and his love for you and your family?

Then, dear moms, keep calm and read on.

Something that is beautiful about the Church is that it holds the mother in high esteem. But the sublimity of motherhood can be a double-edged sword. It's ingrained in us to make mothering a huge part of our lives, to do it well, to give our best. Far too often, women equate giving mothering our best with being perfect.

In the pages that follow, I'll take a look at some of the nagging "earworms" that trip us up and guilt us into doing and saying things that force us into someone else's idea of perfection rather than allowing us to become the people God intended us to be all along. You'll also find group discussion questions at the end of the book that will help you reflect on and share your mothering journey with close friends or a mother's group at your parish. It's my prayer that this book might help all mothers feel worthy of their calling and also reveal how speaking the truth can liberate us from the myriad fears that may prevent us from being the good parents we so desperately long to be. Our fears prevent us from becoming the truest versions of ourselves. Likewise, our fears are inextricably linked to a lack of trust in our God.

Authentic motherhood cannot be rooted in fear; it must come from a place of love and trust.

Few of life's pursuits can cause more of a barrage of self-doubt, guilt, and exhaustion than mothering. But it's my hope that by opening up about my own struggles as a mother and what has helped me to deal with them, I'll help to free other moms to change the ways they see their own mothering, to be willing to grow imperfectly, and to lessen mom guilt: the guilt that we're not the moms we should be; the guilt that we're the only moms who daydream about running away from it all; the guilt that we could and should do more and be more. In place of that heap of guilt, I want to assure you that through God's grace, love, and endless stream of mercy, each of us is exactly the mom our children need us to be.

CHAPTER 1

Queen Mommy

MOTHERHOOD IS NOT THE MOST IMPORTANT JOB A WOMAN HAS

EVIL EARWORM

Being a mother is the *most important thing* a Catholic woman can do.

UNVARNISHED TRUTH

Motherhood is actually not your highest calling. Being a daughter of God is.

When some people find out how many children I have, they're quick to canonize me Saint Mommy. "You must be so patient," I've heard on more than one occasion. Amazingly, these same commentators seem impervious to the sideways glances and eye rolls from my children who have just witnessed someone use the words "patient" and "mom" in the same sentence when referring to their own mother. I'm a lot of things: fun, energetic, creative, passionate, witty, and athletic, but patience is not my best virtue. I've had to really work hard at cultivating patience as a mom, and I wouldn't even call myself one of those women who was, by nature, going to organically evolve into a mother.

On the contrary, my own call to motherhood came more abruptly than slowly and naturally. As a teenager and young woman, I didn't have a strong desire to be a mother—at least not for a long time. I had places to go and things to do! What's more, I wasn't a particularly nurturing child. I bossed my younger brother around, prayed for the rapture when I was relegated to the kids' table at family gatherings and put in charge of overseeing the little ones, and decided to trade in my babysitting jobs for jean folder extraordinaire at the GAP as soon as I snagged my driver's license. Babies and kids were cute enough, and I imagined that probably one day—way, way, way in the future—I'd be ready to settle down and get married and have a family, but first things first!

After being accepted into law school, I took a clerk job at a posh law firm in the city. One morning as I was commuting to work, I experienced what can only be described as a true calling. I was sitting on the subway reading St. Teresa of Calcutta's *A Simple Path*; the now-saint was talking about how charity must begin at home, and an avalanche of strong feelings crashed through me. As I sifted through the emotional sediment, I realized—*what in the world?*—I really, really wanted to be a wife and a mother someday. *Ah-ha! This is what I'm supposed to do with my life.*

Sharing this moment feels a little like seeing a Charlton Heston-like figure appear, surrounded by flocks of chubby cherubs.

Yet at that instant and since then, I've never stopped believing it was a very real spiritual happening when something outside of my own personal whims was at work.

This revelation was both exciting and terrifying—and also odd to me, since I was single at the time and had actually sworn off suitors for more than a year after a particularly bad breakup. But God doesn't call the equipped. He equips the called, and not shortly thereafter, God equipped me with a handsome, nice young man I had known and dated briefly in high school. Said man is now my husband. When we reunited, he was preparing for his own rigorous professional training, so I dropped out of law school, started writing for a living, got married, and promptly began pining for babies.

At the time, I was also delving further into my faith, exploring documents like St. John Paul II's *Letter to Women*. The letter addresses and lauds women from all walks of life, but I zeroed in on what he wrote to women who are physical mothers: "You have sheltered human beings within yourselves in a unique experience of joy and travail. This experience makes you become God's own smile upon the newborn child, the one who guides your child's first steps, who helps it to grow, and who is the anchor as the child makes its way along the journey of life."[1] As a mother, I considered, I would be God's own smile and anchor to my children. This call to motherhood was sublime and a sure path to holiness.

All of this is true, of course, but as I've grown into mothering shoes, I've learned that there's a danger in seeing our roles as mothers as our absolute highest calling.

The more I personally saw my role as a mother as my only and loftiest calling, the more pressure I felt to do everything right. At the same time, other parts of my life were too easily neglected. In my early years of mothering, I wrote about being a mom, read mom blogs and parenting books, joined mom groups, said prayers geared toward mothers, and meticulously tracked my cycle with one thought on my mind—*babies, babies, and more babies!*

Meanwhile, I gave the sometimes-sparse emotional leftovers to the other important relationships in my life—including my personal relationship with God. In my quest to be a godly mother, I had completely isolated myself from God, relegating all energy to my parenting.

THE CORONATION OF MOTHER

I've never been what you'd call a smother mother. My toddlers probably ate more dirt than vegetables. Once I lost three out of four kids at a soccer game. The one I hadn't lost was the one playing on the field. I found the other three dangling precariously from the top of a tree. I made sure they safely returned to the ground, and then I returned to the bleachers to watch the soccer game only to lose the three again. But that doesn't mean I'm not an obsessive mother. Crown me Queen Mommy because *this is the most important job in the world; I will pour everything into it, and I will not screw it up!* I don't worry about scrapes and bruises so much, but there are nights I lie awake terrified that I've ruined my children, that I haven't done enough for them or that I've done too much for them. There have been times when someone has asked me to share my talents for a good purpose, and I've quickly said no because I am a mother—the CEO of Souls Incorporated—and my children need me, all of me, all of the time, thank you very much.

There have also been periods when even my prayer life has suffered. *I don't have time to pray because this mothering assignment and managing a household is all-consuming.* Ironically, however, I always seem to find time to mindlessly peruse Instagram while stirring soup for dinner.

I personally have not had issues with not making my marriage a priority, partly because baby-making includes him, but I know of other mothers who reserve their love and intimacy for their children, leaving their spouses feeling lonely and neglected.

The truth is, I'm not Queen Mommy. I'm not queen anything actually, but I *am* a beloved daughter of God. None of us is deserving of a coronation. Let's leave that to our Blessed Mother. When mothering and our children—like anything else of this world—become our ultimate source of fulfillment, happiness, and identity, they can become a form of idolatry. In the midst of our noble desire to be selfless, good parents, it's easy for Christian mothers to forget a simple but profound truth: the highest calling placed upon our lives is to know and love God with all that we have and all that we are.

I'm grateful the Church elevates motherhood to a beautiful calling, that great leaders of the Church like the late Cardinal József Mindszenty described mothers as the most important people on earth, who build "something more magnificent than any cathedral—a dwelling for an immortal soul, the tiny perfection of her baby's body,"[2] but it's frighteningly easy for a "good, Christian" mother to love and serve her children too exclusively as well as to bury her God-given talents from the rest of the world instead of sharing them and allowing them to bear fruit. It also places a lot of pressure on women who suffer from miscarriages or infertility to think that the ultimate path to holiness is *only* fully achieved through physical motherhood.

The *Catechism of the Catholic Church* says, "The virtue of temperance disposes us to *avoid every kind of excess*" (CCC, 2290). It *is* possible to be excessive in our mothering and to idolize the role of mother. But God can help us keep perspective and balance.

MOTHERS NEVER STOP BEING DAUGHTERS OF GOD

In Genesis, a desperate Rachel cries out, "Give me children or I shall die!" (Gn 30:1). Her desire to be a mother is so strong she would rather die than imagine a childless life. Some women know her supplications well. There are those who struggle with infertility, failed adoptions, and/or repeated miscarriages who may wonder why God hasn't blessed them with (more) children.

Aside from interpreting Rachel's lamentation literally, many moms pour their hearts and souls into mothering as if it is the only thing that matters. In doing so, other parts of their lives wither and die.

There are unquestionably seasons in a mother's life—such as when we have a newborn or many little ones under our roofs or we have a special-needs child in our care—when certain areas of our lives will inevitably have to take a backseat, but nurturing our relationship with God is nonnegotiable.

Our highest calling in this life is not *mother* but *child* of God. No matter how delightful our children are, they were not given to us to fulfill us in a way that only God can. And no matter how our children might disappoint us, we need not be shaken or question ourselves. Our value is attached to our identities as cherished daughters of God. We can all breathe a sigh of relief, accepting that our role as mother is limited but God's love for our children as well as for us is not. This knowledge can free us to love our children as God loves them—not because he craves their attention, not because he needs them to need him, not for what they will offer to him or to do for him, but simply because they belong to him and he was the one who loved them first. We put too much pressure on our children and ourselves if being their mother is what fills us up.

My oldest is only twelve and we have a new baby in our midst, so I have a lot more years to come as a hands-on mom. But even when my last child is no longer in my home or in my arms, I know I'll still have a great purpose. I may end up filling the silence with a chorus of alleluias, but I suspect it will be bittersweet when my nest is finally empty. I also know there will be much more work to do even before the grandchildren, God willing, start to arrive. I am here in this beautiful, broken world to love and know God and to love others—not just the children entrusted to me but every single person I encounter.

This knowledge will make these inevitable valedictions with the children I cherish and love so much a little less difficult.

Secular society warns women against losing their identities in their children, but our children aren't the real identity thieves. They really are the blessings, not the soul-sucking leeches. No, the real identity thieves aren't the children themselves but the ways we may start to view motherhood. If being a mother is your end-all, then you'd better believe it's going to rob you of some of yourself. But if it's a mighty calling but not the *only* calling pressed upon you, you will not become a "nonperson." You were God's daughter first, and you'll always be his beloved. That won't ever change, no matter what season of life you find yourself in.

God invites us to lose ourselves in Christ's life, not in our children's lives. It's not as if carving out prayer time and loving God with our entire beings means we will love our children any less. On the contrary, making our faith life our first priority helps ensure we will love our children not more or less but simply the right way.

Prayer time as a busy mother is rarely going to be of the contemplative variety. Accept that, and pray on. This is your daily bread: interrupted prayer, unfinished sentences, cold coffee. But don't give up, dear mother. God wants any prayer you can offer. He wants *you*. He desires a *relationship* with *you*. There have been many times when I've decided to spend time with my Father, and a hungry child or a sibling squabble has immediately interrupted me. I used to, and sometimes still do, get angry at God or my kids and then feel guilty about it. What I'm trying to learn to do is to take a deep breath and remember that even the disciples followed Jesus when he tried to sneak away and pray. It wasn't always easy for him to escape his everyday tasks, but that didn't mean he stopped trying.

I also love what St. Francis de Sales said about handling interruptions during prayer: "Try interrupting the meditations of someone who is very attached to her spiritual exercises and you will see her upset, flustered, taken aback. A person who has this true freedom will leave her prayer, unruffled, gracious toward the person who has unexpectedly disturbed her, for to her it's all the same—serving God by meditating or serving him by responding to her neighbor. Both are the will of God, but helping the neighbor is necessary at that particular moment."[3] As you fill a thirsty child's cup, ask that God will fill you up, too, and that he will perfect your intentions, that he will help you to make your life a hymn of love to him, and that you will allow the many interruptions faced on any given day to help you to grow in patience and holiness. If you make a mindful effort to remain close to your Father, then you'll be closer to doing what St. Paul instructs us to do: "Pray without ceasing" (1 Thes 5:17).

God seeks you out every single day. As you are. Even if, like me, you're frequently a hot mess who hasn't showered in two days. Being aware of God and his love for you and your family is half the battle.

As your children grow older and aren't so dependent on you, consider deepening your faith in God in other ways. Attend a retreat, spend time in adoration, or join a Bible study. I occasionally spend a few hours away from my children while they're under the competent and compassionate care of grandparents. This is not only a blessing to me but to my children as well. There are other people who can be godly influences on them and love them while I'm MIA. I don't have a monopoly on loving them. There are others who are eager to step in and lend you a hand and wash your children's feet, figuratively or literally.

There's no such thing as "just a mom," whether you work outside of the home or not. You are first and foremost a child of God. Your value and worth are rooted in your identity as one of God's wonderfully made children—not in motherhood or how well you do this mom thing or in anything else worldly for that matter. Be content in your role. Love God with all of your heart and loving your children will become even more natural and life-affirming.

OTHER RELATIONSHIPS IN YOUR LIFE

If you are married, making your relationship with God a priority will also help you to more fully love and appreciate your spouse. It will free you to love and to accept your husband as he is and to leave any big changing that needs to be done in God's hands.

Make extra time this week to express your love for your spouse, even if it's just a few minutes. Offer a back rub, a word of encouragement before he begins his day, an unexpected moment of intimacy. Surprise him by taking care of a dreaded chore or cooking him his favorite meal. Set aside time each evening for conversation. Ask him about his day, his experiences, his joys, and his concerns. And please don't fall into the trap of relying on your husband to take out all of your garbage. I'm not talking about dragging the trash can to the curb. I'm referring to your emotional garbage, your brokenness, your deepest wounds. Your husband loves you very much, but none of us can rely on our spouse or anyone else to heal and satisfy us in a way that only God can.

Nor can we give to our husbands only in order to receive. As St. Teresa of Calcutta said, it's not real love until it hurts. "True love" is really about making the decision to put someone else's needs above your own. This might mean having sex with your husband when you're tired and really and truly do have a headache. He needs that connection and intimacy. Don't hold out on him because you're feeling drained, unfulfilled, or are waiting to enjoy sex more once your abs look better. Your abs are fine; it's the way you see yourself that's holding you back. Yes, you have needs, too, and you must express these needs in a clear, hostile-free manner. Raising kids feels like a thankless job sometimes, and we need love and support to sustain us. But men don't always know what would make us feel loved and appreciated. He's not a mind reader, so tell your husband what makes you feel loved and remind him that you need this kind of love from him regularly.

If your marriage is hurting, or you're just struggling to find time for your spouse because you're at a point in your mothering life that has left you with little else to give, then simply turn to God and pray for peace in your overwhelmed heart. Pray for your marriage and husband as well. Tell him you're struggling, that you're overwhelmed. If you're treading water, he thinks you're fine. Don't wait until you're drowning to issue an SOS. One day the children will be out of the house, but your husband will remain. This relationship needs nurturing and care.

There are other relationships in your life that need tending as well. I'm blessed with some amazing girlfriends. I'm not sure what I would do without them. I have a few close friends who have shown up at my doorstep with meals when we lost our family dog or when I'd just had a hard day. These friends have taken a child off my hands so I could have a moment's peace. I can talk to them about everything from chic shoes to God. I never had a biological sister, but God has blessed me with these sisters in Christ. I can't take these friendships for granted. I have to be grateful for them *and* make time for them.

One of my friends and I have talked about how sad it is that so many of us use the excuse of being too busy to cultivate real friendships. My evenings belong to my family now. This is when I begin the schlepping to sports and make a Herculean effort to eat dinner as a family. I've had to give up my monthly book club night, but I am still very intentional about tending a few of my closest friendships. One of my friends and I wake up at 5:15 a.m. a few times a week to run and talk together. I have other friends who I call a few times a month to catch up. Some neighborhood friends and I get our kids together occasionally and reconnect while they play. I belong to a women's Bible study group as well; I've been able to open up to these women about some of my fears and insecurities, and they have lifted me up with their faith and support. Life is busy, but we must make time for maintaining friendships. I need my girlfriends in my life because they can read me and understand me in a way that my wonderful husband, God bless him, cannot.

Every mother needs key friendships in her life. I'm not talking about countless Facebook friends who share pithy or witty quotes that make you laugh. I'm talking about the friend you could call up in the middle of the night for help or support if you had to, the kind of friend who would sit with you during chemotherapy treatments after you've been diagnosed with cancer. If you're blessed with an inner circle of friends, be grateful and perhaps plan a fun get-together with a girlfriend, or write her a note expressing your love for her and why you're so glad to have her in your life. If you find yourself pining for an authentic friend—the kind you'd never have to clean your house for—pray about how you might find her.

CHARITY MUST BEGIN AT HOME, BUT IT NEEDN'T STOP THERE

St. Teresa of Calcutta was right: charity begins at home. But I'm learning that it sometimes must extend beyond the reaches of our doorsteps. It *is* possible to serve our children and family too exclusively, to squander our God-given gifts, and to ignore our greater purposes as his disciples.

I've wanted to work on a book about motherhood for a long time, but what kept me from starting to write was the feeling that I was being selfish and also wasn't the best expert on mothering, considering a neighbor once called me and asked if I knew my son was in the front yard pooping. (I didn't.) Truthfully, aside from my lackluster skill set as an übermom, I felt like there was no longer time to write and that my only purpose was to serve my family. Yet I missed connecting with like-minded women, and I'd get this divine prodding every once in a while that God wanted me to be a little pencil in his hand, as St. Teresa of Calcutta once described.

One day the local parochial school invited me to be a guest author for their family reading night since I'd previously published *Weightless*.[4] A reception was held in my honor, and I honestly felt sheepish attending. During the event, a teacher who taught one of my daughters came up to me and said, "Do you know how proud Madeline is of you? She talks about her 'mom the author' all the time."

Another one of my daughters frequently says she wants to be a writer "like you, Mommy" (and an ethologist, animal trainer, singer, etc. Shoot for the moon, and you'll fall among the stars, right?).

Encounters like this leave me humbled as well as enlightened. My children may not notice that I'm always doing laundry, but they know I write and have other talents that I try to give to the glory of God. Children don't just want mothers who are excited to have them in their lives; they want and benefit from having moms who are excited about their own lives. Don't our children deserve to witness us using our gifts and doing what we do best? Some of our talents might not make us rich, or any money at all, but they are still worthy of our time. Our children will pick up on the fact that we have the capacity for encouraging—but only if we make it a habit to encourage others. Just as we see the genius in our children's scribbles, they will glimpse the genius in the way we write, speak our minds, nurture friendships, or open our homes and hearts to others.

As wives and mothers, we have the responsibility to place ourselves in the service of our families first, but God has a divine purpose for each of us, and there are good works he calls us to do—both inside and outside of the home.

We can't do it all, at least not at the same time, and there's absolutely nothing wrong with being "only" an at-home mom. Just like you can't fit everything you want to eat on one dinner plate, there's no way we can do everything we want to do, are called to do, need to do, and dream of doing in one single season.

Is it fair? Maybe not. But we only have so much energy to go around—and so many hours in a day. And anything that we want to do well takes both time and the wholehearted support of those around us. Sometimes, many times even, you will have to say no, but please remember that behind every no (even when you have to turn down something good and worthwhile) is a yes to your family. When we say yes to the people God has entrusted to us, we're saying yes to him. It all comes full circle, then. We are God's beloved daughters. He loved us first. Now we show our love to him by loving others well.

Mom's Time-Out

My heavenly Father, help me to remember always that I am first and foremost your beloved daughter. I am your handiwork, created in Jesus Christ for the good works you have prepared in advance for me (see Eph 2:10). Please help me to discover and cultivate my gifts to do your good works. I know I'll be able to more closely follow your will if I pray more and draw closer to you with every breath I take. We become more like the people we spend the most time with, and I want to become like you. I want to share your love not only with my children but with my spouse, my friends, my extended family, my coworkers, my parish community, the mail carrier, the stranger at the mall—with every single person I encounter in my life. Keep knocking on my heart, reminding me that loving my children is not enough. I have to love you with all of my soul and all of my mind and love others as I love myself (see Mt 22:37–39). Amen.

Mary lost herself in love. This doesn't mean she suffered an identity loss or forfeited her personality. Instead, her personality, her identity, her life—these were purified through God. She didn't need to do anything ostentatious. When she visited Elizabeth, she didn't have to say anything. She was the first eucharistic procession. Her presence alone made the child in Elizabeth's womb leap for joy. Elizabeth and her son, John, saw Jesus in Mary. When you abandon yourself to God, others will see Jesus in you as well. Today, pray a Hail Mary and ask to be a handmaid to the Lord.

CHAPTER 2

I Love Motherhood— Except When I Don't

YOU'RE NOT SUPPOSED TO ENJOY EVERY MOMENT

EVIL EARWORM

You're supposed to enjoy every moment of motherhood. Something's wrong with you if you don't feel love for your kids every waking hour.

UNVARNISHED TRUTH

Motherhood is the toughest job you'll ever (sometimes) love, and your kids sometimes will drive you crazy. That doesn't make you a bad mom. It makes you a normal mom. Biblical love is very, very difficult to live out.

One fine morning I had the brilliant idea to gather four kids, who were all under age seven, and emerge from our safe hole where sporting face crust and wearing pajamas all day are perfectly acceptable behaviors. We had plans to meet a friend and her two children for lunch at an indoor food court.

I tucked my four-month-old into a baby carrier, held my four-year-old and two-year-old's hands, and asked my seven-year-old to not skip too far ahead, and we entered the real world.

Lunch was not too catastrophic. My patient, generous friend helped out a lot when she wasn't busy juggling her own two littles.

We sort of caught up with one another in fragmented sentences. "So how are you? . . . Stop poking your sister!"

"Life is busy but good. What about you? . . . Watch out! You almost spilled your drink."

Despite the constant interruptions, I was thinking it was nice to be out and about wearing chic clothes—even if my baby had slobbered all over me. I felt quasi-human.

I wasn't planning on shopping after lunch. I just wanted to quickly return something since I rarely made it out to a mall. I forgot that doing anything *quickly* is impossible when you're managing so many little ones out in public. My seven-year-old, for reasons I still cannot explain, started repeatedly hurling herself onto the ground.

"Why are you doing that?" I asked.

"I'm tired."

"Well, if you're too tired to walk, then you're too tired to have a sleepover with your friend," I said. (My friend was planning on taking my daughter back with her for a slumber party.)

She instantly popped up and began skittering about with more energy than a hummingbird.

Sigh of relief from me. But that was the baby's cue to start wailing.

"It's time to go," I announced. "Rachel, do you have to go to the bathroom?"

"No," my four-year-old replied.

"Are you sure?"

"Yes!" she answered emphatically.

So we headed to the exit, exchanged good-byes, and I was about to congratulate myself for surviving the trip when Rachel tugged my hand, "Mommy, I told you I had to go to the bathroom."

"No, you didn't," I said.

"YES! I DID," my feudal lord screeched.

I repeated the conversation we'd just had, and she burst into tears. "You don't understand," she said. "I told you I was *sure* I had to go to the bathroom."

Huh?

Okay, so we'll traipse back to the bathroom. No biggie. I can handle this.

We returned inside the mall. Rachel was still sobbing, wondering why she was so unlucky to have such an obtuse, uncaring mom who could not begin to understand her. Baby was crying, too, and burrowing deeper and deeper into my chest. My entire body was tingling from the effusive milk letdown I was experiencing.

Then my two-year-old decided to go limp. *Wonderful.*

I tried to pick her up, but that's not easy when you have a tank-of-a-baby-boy barnacled to you, and you're trying to console an emotional four-year-old. So I started to drag her across the floor of the mall. People were staring. A few understanding moms smiled sympathetically at me. But then a teenage boy with a horrible Justin Bieber hairdo had to crush my already withering spirit by remarking as we passed by, "Man, that kid's getting dragged."

In that instant, I wanted to grab that wisp of a boy, stare him down, and say, "You have no idea! Your biggest problem is Snapchat malfunctions!" I wanted to burst into tears like my four-year-old and nestle into the chest of my husband or even my own mom like my baby was doing. I even considered that

going limp and being slid across the floor—gently, I should add—
would be better than what I was being forced to endure at that
very moment.

Instead, I gathered my resolve and dragged myself, my
floppy child, and the baby I was wearing to the bathroom while
my four-year-old shuffled tearfully behind.

Then I started to laugh. It was an uncontrollable fit of giggles
that gurgled inside of me and would not be contained. I laughed
all the way back to the minivan, still lugging my motley, madden-
ing crew behind me. Once in my car, I text-vented my husband,
and he responded, "That sounds awful. I'm glad you survived."
I convulsed with laughter like a mad, uncaring mother, and then
I started the hour drive home.

All my kids fell asleep, and that's when some of the laughter—all of those big emotions—ebbed, and I wondered why
mothering could be such a crappy job sometimes. I wasn't even
dealing with worrying about where our next meal would come
from, a sick child, or another big mothering challenge. I was simply trying to manage the sheer exhaustion, the everyday defiance
and baby spit-up, and the endless outpouring of patience and
love when sometimes all I wanted to do was scream at my kids.

There are some days when I do yell. There are days when
my kids drive me absolutely crazy. During a particularly rough
patch, I would frequently lock myself in the bathroom just to
catch the smallest pocket of peace. One day after I took a deep
breath and reentered the fray, my oldest patted me on the back
and said, "Mommy, I'm so sorry you're so constipated." Busted.

On a really bad day, I may or may not have entertained the
leave-it-all-behind fantasy of running away from it all in the middle of the night and somewhat gleefully imagining the chaos in
my home and all the broken hearts of my family when they discovered Mommy had disappeared. I bet they wouldn't complain
about Mom having taco salad *again* on Tuesday night then!

GNATS

When I became pregnant with my first child, I could not imagine ever *not* loving motherhood or feeling a sugary-sweet affection for my baby. The feel-good hormones of childbirth, nursing, and early motherhood worked well on me with my first child. I didn't immediately understand the feelings of inadequacy or even resentment that would eventually pulse through me.

When I was still pregnant with my first child, I was checking out baby gear in Target when I saw a toddler tugging his mother's shirt while asking "Why?" over and over. I found the encounter completely endearing until the mother snapped, "I don't know why. Would you stop pulling on my shirt like that!"

I reflexively placed my hand on my burgeoning belly and thought to myself, *I will never squelch your curiosity, little one. You can always ask why and hold on to me.*

Fast-forward to more than a decade later. My eight-year-old is asking me what box turtles eat. I am trying to get food on the table after soccer practice and before my youngest has a low-blood-sugar meltdown. I hiss, "I don't know. Go google it."

"But I'm not allowed to google by myself," she whined.

"We'll figure it out later," I said. And we did, but I certainly hadn't been the most attentive mother to my daughter's curious question.

I remember reading the novel *Ladder of Years* before I had any children and being miffed at the heroine's selfish behavior. In the Anne Tyler book, fifty-year-old Delia Grinstead strolls down a shoreline and just keeps walking, abandoning her husband and three older children. The decision is not a premeditated one, and there was no big fight or breaking point that forced her to walk away from it all. She leaves more on an impulsive whim because she is tired of feeling like a "tiny gnat buzzing around her family's edges."[1]

I could not empathize with Delia's sudden, self-serving behavior back then. Today I have more insight. As my children grow older, I now sometimes feel like that gnat, too—the one everyone is swatting away and doesn't want around to bug them about picking up dirty laundry off the floor or being kind to their siblings. Or, I admit, there are moments when I feel like my children are the gnats and *won't they please just leave me alone for ten flippin' seconds!*

And that's when the guilt bubbles over in my heart, and I wonder, "What kind of mother am I? That my kids sometimes drive me crazy? That I don't always love being their mother?"

MOTHERHOOD IS SUPPOSED TO MAKE US HAPPY AND FULFILLED, RIGHT?

I love my children fiercely. I also frequently love being a mother, but there are many days when I don't. And that used to really bother me. From the moment I first felt the call to motherhood, I viewed it as a path to fulfillment and happiness. As someone who is passionately pro-life and considers children a godsend, I buried the cell-deep feeling that something was wrong with me because I sometimes wanted, like the fictitious Delia, to run away from it all.

My belief that motherhood was supposed to make me happy led me to spend one entire year denying I could possibly have postpartum depression. After my third baby, I skipped my post-partum six-week checkup. *I was fine. There was no time for that.* Holding my beautiful baby, I was so deluded in hope and happiness that I became overwhelmed by the realization of how scary, lonely, and heartbreaking motherhood can sometimes be. I'd wander out to the grocery store with three little ones, and people would "*Oooh*" and "*Ahhh,*" telling me to savor and enjoy these years because they would fly by quickly and that these years were simply the best.

Were they? I wondered in the middle of the night when I was alone with a crying infant. We'd been this way, night after night, the two of us. Her tears and whimpering would start, and then I would join her; we'd have our nightly cry-along, and I would be left feeling disillusioned, wondering why the gift of motherhood felt like anything but a gift during these lonely moments.

Then a few months later, after I'd finally sought help for what was diagnosed as postpartum depression, I was flipping through an old high school scrapbook when I remembered people saying very similar things to me about savoring my young adulthood and enjoying every moment of it and me feeling disheartened as I clumsily teetered on the edge of childhood and adulthood, wobbling in one direction and then the other, feeling totally unbalanced. It dawned on me that just as our culture encourages young people to "find themselves"—to "eat, pray, and love" on their own terms in order to find happiness—we have come to expect motherhood to fill us with contentment and pleasure.

No one is more guilty of candy-coating motherhood than the Christian community. In our plight to protect the sanctity of life and promote family values, we have elevated motherhood as a means to an end. All that worldly, "selfish" stuff won't make you happy, but becoming a mother will. Children are no longer only blessings; they become tools to etch out our own gratification. Because we rightfully respect mothers so much, perhaps we have over-glorified the view of motherhood. We all need a savior. But motherhood isn't it. Just as culture idealizes romantic love and tells us it's all about feel-good feelings, it's easy for us to fall into the trap of believing that motherhood is supposed to make us *feel* good when, maybe, it's intended to help us to learn to *be* and *do* good.

Whenever we hear stories about people choosing child-free lives or mothers who openly admit they regret having children, there's an almost instant wave of Christian backlash. People who don't have kids—or even what we might see as "enough" children—are sometimes viewed as chasing after fleeting things such as travel and money that surely won't bring lasting happiness. We may accuse them of ignoring the eternal value of bringing children into the world.

But don't some of us Christian parents desire children for some selfish reasons, too? We're not just making the decision to have children because we're all selfless do-gooders. Most people aspire to have children because we assume having a family will help to make us happy, fulfill us, reveal God's parental and unconditional love to us, and maybe even get us a one-way ticket to heaven since caring for children requires sacrificial love. It could be argued that we have our own set of self-serving motivations for having children.

Have we traded one error for another? We live in a culture that is fixated on pursuing our own pleasures, and as Christ-followers, we rightly swim upstream against the tide of seeking worldly things such as popular acclaim or a closet full of designer clothing. We've eschewed more meaningless things in exchange for raising children. But then, when we struggle or find it difficult, we decide that something must be wrong with us or with our children or that maybe we're not praying enough, when in reality, the only thing that's flawed with us is that we've lost sight of the big picture.

WHO SAID MOTHERHOOD IS EASY?

Motherhood is not a prison sentence, but it's no walk in the park, either. And maybe, dear sisters in Christ, that's the whole point. I've joked with friends that if a mother says her job is easy then either she has boring kids or she's lying.

Many of us *are tempted* to lie about the challenges of motherhood and the reality that it doesn't always make us happy because we're afraid about what that says of us as our children's moms and as Christians.

Several years ago I was resting in bed with a hot compress, thanks to my first case of mastitis, when I received an e-mail from a friend who was a new mom to multiples. She openly admitted she was really struggling to find joy in motherhood. Reading her honest words pierced my heart because I know what it's like to

feel overwhelmed and to find yourself in a dark place instead
of basking in baby bliss. Postpartum depression robs you of the
joy of those sweet, early weeks of motherhood. Yet even when
you don't have to deal with depression or the baby blues, if you
expect to be happy every day during those early weeks of motherhood—or during any phase of motherhood—you're setting
yourself up for disappointment.

"Being a mom is so hard," my friend confided.

No doubt about that, I thought as I looked down at my swollen,
burning breast.

We're fooling ourselves if we try to make being a mom out to
be entirely sepia-toned *all of the time.* We're also depriving ourselves of the real gift of motherhood. We cannot link our levels of
happiness to the value of motherhood. The reason being a mother
is so incredibly worthwhile—aside from those sweet moments
we all have when we do feel incredible love and affection for our
children—is because of just how hard it is.

I had another new-mom friend ask me a few years back why
no one had ever told her how tough those first few months would
be. She was on a never-ending cycle of feeding, sleeping, and
changing diapers, and she felt cut off from the rest of the world.

Then there's a friend of mine who is way beyond the baby
stage and is actually pining for those sleepless nights because at
least she could comfort her whimpering wee ones by holding
them close. Now that her kids are teens, they're often aloof, and
she feels like she can't connect with them. Recently, another dear
friend confessed to me that she just seesaws between feeling list-
less and angry when she's dealing with her rambunctious boys.

I ache for all these moms. And it's not a physical, mastitis
ache but a visceral one. No one had to tell me how hard motherhood was going to be. I discovered it all on my own.

It's a different kind of hard, too. It's not brain surgery hard,
though I've obviously never performed brain surgery. Motherhood isn't about perfect precision or highly specialized training

or expertise, although the way so many of us moms are laser-beam focused on our children might have you think otherwise.

It's not marathon hard either. Training for and running a marathon is difficult, but I've done it before, and you *can* train for covering all those miles. Your body miraculously adapts, and it's only yourself you have to convince to move forward. You're not dealing with one or more humans with purpose who frequently offer nothing but incessant insubordination to thwart your every move. And yes, 26.2 miles is long, but you'll cross the finish line in no more than a few hours, even if you're the slowest of the pack. Then it's time to celebrate. You finished the race. Labor might be a little like a marathon because the baby will come sooner rather than later, but not day-to-day mothering. That's different. Harder. Longer.

Is there ever a finish line to cross as a mother? My mom says even though her children are grown and all on their own, she thinks about them throughout her day. When one of us is hurt or faces a disappointment or a health scare, her mama bear instinct kicks in. She wants to protect and heal, but she's often powerless to do anything. That's an altogether different kind of hard than the sheer exhaustion I have faced being a mother to little ones.

Motherhood is not a sprint, and it's not even a marathon. It's the ultimate extreme sport. There's potential for danger. Toddlers constantly try to kill themselves. Babies scratch your eye in the middle of the night, resulting in a corneal abrasion (one of the many casualties I have suffered as a mama). There's the risk of loving and not getting much or anything in return.

But there's a different kind of danger, too. There's the danger in telling yourself being a mom is only hard for *you*. Or worse, that this mothering business is tough work because there's something wrong with *you*. Don't believe you possess some personal defect because you're feeling alone, sad, angry, frustrated, frazzled, and burned out, or because your kids sometimes get on your nerves, or because you didn't instantly bond with your baby, or because your teens constantly roll their eyes at you.

Being a mother is hard for us all. In different ways, perhaps, but it's not all roses and sunshine for any of us. Being a new mother is hard. Being a mom of one or three or seven is hard. Being a mom of tiny tyrants is hard, but so is mothering teens and even young and older adults.

Moms, don't be too weary if you're traveling down a difficult path right now in your parenting journey. Don't wonder if you're the only one who finds a newborn baby, toddler, preschooler, seven-year-old, tween, teenager, young adult, grown child, special-needs child, girl, boy—whatever kind of child is in your midst—difficult to mother. Because you're not the only one. Wherever you're at and whatever you've been given right now is probably the hardest for you. Maybe that's the point. What would be easy for you may not be the best for you. God gifts us with children—whether biologically or through adoption—not only because we are creatures of love and have an innate desire to share this love but because we need to be taught *how* to love. And children are very good teachers in lessons of real love— the kind that isn't a feeling but a daily, or sometimes, it feels, by-the-second, decision. We're no better than secularists if we make happiness in parenting our highest goal.

If God is trying to prune us and sanctify us through the vocation of parenthood then it makes sense that he gives us just the kind of children we need—the kind who will push our buttons and throw us down to our knees and force us to realize that we cannot, absolutely cannot, do this on our own. We need good girlfriends we can vent to. We need spouses or other loved ones to lean on. We need community. We need to take care of ourselves to better take care of those entrusted to us. And we need faith. Faith is what makes our weakness—whether it's spiritual, physical, or emotional—stronger. We have to have faith that this will pass, that we *will* survive. We also have to have the faith that even when raising children brings more frustration than fulfillment, it is a worthy calling.

Sometimes we have to simply show up—and to stay put once we've arrived, even if every part of us is screaming to just go, escape, get the heck out of there before we or our children really lose it.

Biblical, sacrificial love doesn't come easy for any of us. Neither does letting go of our own power, our own agendas, as well as our old lives. Mothering requires us to do all of these things and to do them when we're often skimping on sleep or even good nutrition. Surely our bodies deserve more than grazing on our children's leftover bread crusts.

The first step to being a more peaceful mother, for me, was to recognize and accept that motherhood isn't supposed to be easy or to make me feel happy all of the time. God intended it to make me holy. Just because children are valuable and a blessing doesn't mean they're supposed to feel like a reward—like a pampering pedicure at the end of a long week. How we *feel* about our children at any given moment isn't a measure of our or their worth or our love for them.

To all moms, I'll say this: what you're doing is extreme, and it demands exceptional energy, love, and faith. It will sometimes leave you crying for joy, but there will be plenty of times where you'll be crying in despair or frustration or worse.

As a mom, you're certain to acquire some hurt, some aches, and some bruises. There may even be more hurt than happiness in the trenches of motherhood. You'll sometimes become a suffering servant, and that's where you'll find Christ—in your wounds.

There will be tears, tantrums, wayward children, and bathroom hideouts. There will be days you wish you could erase. There will be holes in your children's lives—some of them gaping—that you alone cannot fill.

But as with a seed buried beneath the wintertime earth, it is in the dark spaces where the growth begins to happen.

You will never be the same. Loving your children will cost you. Don't be afraid to admit this, to embrace this. Motherhood isn't happy hour or Pinterest-perfect.

It's okay to be afraid, dear Mama, but it's also necessary to recognize this giving and changing and becoming as a good thing, a beautiful thing.

Being a mother may not always or ever be the source of your joy, but like Mama Mary, it very well may become the *cause* of your joy. Motherhood breaks you only to build you into the woman you were meant to become: a woman who is neither too hard nor too soft, an exceptional woman who is strong without having sharp edges, a holy woman.

A mother doesn't have superhero powers or even super patience. A mother is just a person, but she does super-amazing things. She is the woman with people in her care whom she loves and who sometimes wonders how she loves them because they're driving her absolutely crazy. Yet she still chooses love. She gives; she fights, prays, and works. She shows up day after day for what sometimes feels like a thankless or even pointless job. And it's in this showing up, minute after minute, hour after hour, day after day that just may make a mother a saint.

Mom's Time-Out

Dear God, please use my children and my love for them as a way to mold me more into the image of your Son. You gave me these children not simply because I had the desire to love but because I needed to be taught how to love. Every day my children instruct me, humble me, bring me to my knees, and remind me that I'm nothing more than a beggar for you and your graces. Help me to remember that being a faithful parent is more important than always being a happy parent. I pray that I may find joy in my mothering, but

when I don't, remind me to look to you because you
are the only one who can fill the God-shaped hole in
my heart. You are the source of my joy. Amen.

Love—especially sacrificial, biblical love—doesn't always come easy. Try to choose love only for the moment rather than telling yourself you will love with patience and kindness always and forever as a mother. Whenever you're having a hard time feeling love or even expressing it for your children or for your vocation of motherhood, pray an Act of Love:

> O my God, I love you above all things, with my whole heart and soul, because you are all good and worthy of all my love. I love my neighbor as myself for the love of you. I forgive all who have injured me, and I ask pardon of all whom I have injured. Amen.

CHAPTER 3

Perfectionism, Supermom's Kryptonite

BEING IMPERFECT IS ALL THAT IS EXPECTED OF YOU

EVIL EARWORM

God created you to be the *perfect* mom
to *perfect* children. You'd better not
screw up your precious progeny.

UNVARNISHED TRUTH

God created you to be an imperfect human being
who never stops seeking a *perfect* union with him.

Women—and moms, in particular—are experts in pursuing the Holy Grail of perfection. We want always to be good, do good, and have good children.

The pursuit of perfection might not seem like such a bad thing. After all, in many ways it's what drives us to excel and to take care of our homes, our children, our husbands, and sometimes even ourselves, although kind, gentle self-care is often relegated to the "only if I have a whole lot of extra time" portion of the to-do list.

Perfectionists do tend to be a dependable, productive lot. We get things done. We make things happen, or we will die trying to make things—such as potty training or lovely family Christmas photos—happen.

But what are the intentions behind our perfectionistic pursuits? Are we more worried about what others think of us than of our own and our family's sanity and inner peace?

MUFFIN MADNESS

Shortly after I had popped out my fourth baby, I was frantically cluttering my kitchen counters with a myriad of wholesome ingredients to whip up a batch of healthy, made-from-scratch muffins. Meanwhile, my newborn was nestled close to me in a baby carrier and starting to whimper. He was getting hungry, and if I didn't hurry up and beat the nursing clock, the whimpers would turn into full-blown screeching hysteria.

My husband, Dave, wandered into the kitchen and found me stirring ingredients together in a frenzy while gently bouncing the baby to keep him from completely losing it.

"What are you doing?" Dave asked.

"What does it look like I'm doing?" I snapped.

Be easy on me. I'm getting by on five hours of fractured sleep. "I'm making muffins to bring to soccer. It's our turn to bring snacks for the team."

Dave looked at my crazed eyes, askew hair, manic baby bouncing, and then kindly pointed out that maybe we should just bring Goldfish.

I bristled at his counsel. "I've got this," I said, although the circles under my eyes and my involuntary sighing and near swearing suggested otherwise.

He then came over and embraced me, preventing me from bouncing the baby, who began to bleat more loudly. "My love," he said gently, quietly, almost in a whisper. "Maybe you need to get over yourself."

I shrugged his arms off and returned to furious baking-bouncing.

At first, his comment made me angry. *Get over myself? I am doing this for my child and her soccer team!*

Dave offered to hold our baby. I said nothing, but I unstrapped the little guy and handed him over.

Then I grumbled and huffed and puffed for a bit, but as I mixed the batter, I realized Dave was on to something. I wasn't baking those muffins out of love. I was being vain—I needed to secure the approval of others.

As a new mom, I was exhausted, but I didn't want anyone else to know *that*. My finite energy needed to be relegated to the child I'd given birth to a few weeks ago, not a huddle of young soccer players who'd likely spit out the wholesome muffins any-way. Still, I wanted all those other soccer moms to think I had it all together and would only offer the most wholesome goodies to their children. Whereas my husband, bless him, was more concerned with being wise than impressive.

Baking is something I enjoy, and it often *is* done out of love, but when I pull out the mixer, I need to make sure I'm not doing it out of vanity. My heart needs to be in the right place. On that particular day, it wasn't. I was hell-bent on making homemade muffins out of vanity, pride, and fear of the other parents seeing me for what I was at that very moment: a tapped out hot mess who reeked of Eau du Breast Milk.

Since I'd already started making the muffins, I ended up bringing them to the soccer game that day. And lo and behold, a fellow mom remarked, "I don't know how you do it all," but instead of her awe impacting me like a narcotic hit of delight to my eggshell ego, I sheepishly shook my head and told her the truth.

"You should have seen me making these stupid muffins. I was a freak show," I laughed. "Next time I'm bringing Goldfish."

The mom smiled and laughed right along with me. And would you believe that we connected more over the very thing I feared revealing (my imperfect truth) than my sparkly, pretend world where homemade muffins are always a joy to make?

It turns out most moms are grateful for imperfect authenticity. Instead of being rejected and isolated—what I fear might happen if I put my imperfect self out there—I'm embraced when I admit how hard mothering can be. When we let our guard down and stop trying to hide behind a fake façade, others can see us for who we really are.

We are real moms doing our best. Maybe your life is messy and not always (ever?) Pinterest-worthy. But you put yourself out there. You might not do big things. You do mom things—you pack lunches, you fold and fold and fold laundry, you monitor e-mail usage of older kids, kiss boo-boos, wipe sticky counters, read storybooks, and hide away in the bathroom when you need a moment's peace. But these little things add up. Even the hiding-away-in-the-bathroom part because how else will your children learn to solve their own problems? All those little actions and decisions make a difference in your children's lives. They are enough. *You* are enough.

When we accept ourselves as we are and refuse to pretend with anyone, we can find much more joy and contentment in our mothering because we feel good enough just as we are. Our children deserve the same: freedom from the tyranny of our parental image of how they should be and behave.

A young mom of an eighteen-month-old confided in me, "Sometimes I see my toddler's behavior as a direct reflection of my parenting. This toddler stage can be rough. I have to remind myself that my daughter won't and sometimes can't follow all my directions, requests, and begging, but that's just because she's not developmentally there yet."

A toddler who doesn't follow directions, who goes crazy over the weirdest things—socks that don't line up just right on the toes, the color purple—is not bad or insane. She's a toddler. And she's human. The same can be true of eye-rolling, rebelling older children.

So often we measure our children's virtue by what is seen by others and what is avoided for the sake of holiness. We vigilantly monitor media. We teach manners. We preach chastity and purity. But in all our doing, we forget to just trust God and his plan for the children he loves so much in spite of their flaws and transgressions. Does your pink-haired teen love Jesus? That's enough for now. Our perfect parenting expectations are seldom met.

Truth is, very few of us will ever pass the Perfect Parent Test. God is the only perfect parent there is, and let's take a look at *his* children—you and imperfect me, all his offspring who have questioned him, those who crucified his only Son, and then all those who have committed abhorrent acts of genocide, bride burning, and other horrifying crimes of hate. One look at this Father's broken people, and you'd think he has failed miserably as a parent. So why, then, do we take our own children's behavior and choices and imperfections as an indictment of our own parenting? Like many moms, I'm tempted to see my maternal missteps as global pronouncements of my failure to nurture my children right. Why do we put this kind of pressure on ourselves? Why do we try so hard to be perfect? Because we're afraid. Because we lack trust in God and his limitless love for us.

POWER MADE PERFECT IN WEAKNESS

A relentless pursuit of perfection is inextricably linked to fear. Fear of failure. Fear of unpopularity and rejection. Fear of losing control. Fear of people seeing the skeletons and dust bunnies and mismatched shoes hiding in the closet.

Perfectionism is not the same as striving for excellence.

Brené Brown, author of *The Gifts of Imperfection: Let Go of Who You Think You're Supposed to Be and Embrace Who You Are*, draws a sharp distinction between healthy self-improvement and perfectionism:

> *Perfectionism is* not *self-improvement*. Perfectionism is, at its core, about trying to earn approval and acceptance. Most perfectionists were raised being praised for achievement and performance (grades, manners, rule-following, people-pleasing, appearance, sports). Somewhere along the way, we adopt this dangerous and debilitating belief system: I am what I accomplish and how well I accomplish it. *Please. Perform. Perfect.* Healthy striving is self-focused—*How can I improve?* Perfectionism is other-focused—*What will they think?* . . .
>
> Perfectionism is a hustle.
>
> *Perfectionism is self-destructive simply because there is no such thing as perfect. Perfection is an unattainable goal. Additionally, perfectionism is more about perception—we want to be perceived as perfect. Again, this is unattainable—there is no way to control perception, regardless of how much time and energy we spend trying.*
>
> *Perfectionism is addictive because when we invariably do experience shame, judgment, and blame, we often believe it's because we weren't perfect enough. So rather than questioning the faulty logic of perfectionism, we become even*

more entrenched in our quest to live, look, and do everything just right.

Feeling shamed, judged, and blamed (and the fear of these feelings) are realities of the human experience. Perfectionism actually increases the odds that we'll experience these painful emotions and often leads to self-blame: It's my fault. I'm feeling this way because "I'm not good enough."[1]

From my experience, perfectionism is also the ultimate way of playing God. He is perfect. We're not. God didn't design us as super-humans. We are humans who depend upon supernatural grace. He *wants* us to need him. Overcoming perfectionism demands that we acknowledge our flaws, our weaknesses, without any shame and then surrender them as well as everything else to God.

You are enough exactly as you are. Your self-worth is not tied to others' opinions of you or how well your children behave at a restaurant. I show up to social events, and my kids sometimes look like ragamuffins. Does Jesus care if my children's hair looks like a china doll's corn silk strands or whether we contribute store-bought cupcakes instead of homemade fondant concoctions to the school potluck? Nope. Not one iota. He wants our love, and he wants us to share love with others.

At the heart of overcoming perfectionism is not worrying about what others think of you as well as recognizing that you are good enough just the way you are, just the way God designed you to be, and showing the same compassion you give yourself to others. Praying, leaning on other faith-filled women, and working hard to be a good mother, wife, and person is important, but you don't have to change who you are at your core or get in a fight with your daughter over hair just to please some superficial ninny.

What often prevents God's grace from working in our lives is less our sins or failings than it is our failure to accept our own weaknesses—all those rejections, conscious or not, of what we really are or of our real situations. We have to set grace free in our lives by accepting the parts of ourselves that we want to perfect, hide, or reject. Fr. Jacques Philippe, a favorite spiritual writer of mine, puts it this way: "We must accept ourselves just as we are, if the Holy Spirit is to change us for the better."[2]

Remember what Paul writes in Corinthians, that Jesus' "grace is sufficient for you, for power is made perfect in weakness" (2 Cor 12:9). You are blanketed in grace. Don't shut him out by covering up imperfect you and by pursuing the crème de la crème—whether it's with your mothering, your career, your appearance, or your home. Try to shift the focus from what you can and cannot do to what God *can* do *through* you—even through your weaknesses.

Fr. Philippe also writes that we must give ourselves the freedom to be sinners. He explains, "The freedom to be sinners doesn't mean we are free to sin without worrying about the consequences—that would not be freedom but irresponsibility. It means we are not crushed by the fact of being sinners—we have a sort of 'right' to be poor, the right to be what we are."[3]

A sweet friend of mine once opened up to me about the "terrible things" she had done as a mother. She didn't give any details, but she assured me they were far worse than anything I'd ever done. She clearly hadn't witnessed my worst mothering moments. For example, one school year I made an embarrassing mental and parental gaffe in front of my youngest child's patient preschool teachers. At pickup, my son went limp and was asking about watching television and if he could have a cookie and then play with his new laser guns, obviously making me look like a strong contender for Worst Mommy of the Year. When I told him no to all of his requests, he proceeded to kick me from his supine position. I desperately wanted to hightail it out of there and had meant to say, "I'll pick you up now." Instead, I said very loudly in front of Thomas's two teachers—as well as all the other moms who were as cool and as collected as their compliant children,

"I'm going to hit you now." My face flamed red as I tried to correct my words, but everyone knew what I was thinking—*you are making me so mad I want to hit you*—except for Thomas, who didn't seem daunted in the least and remained a thrashing pile of preschool boy bulk on the ground.

I told my anxious friend about another time in my mothering past that still haunts me, a time when I was unkind and horrible to a sweet, beloved child of mine. My daughter had created a huge mess during an act of disobedience. I reacted uncharitably, and I immediately felt awful. Even after Confession, I was still feeling wretched. I was unable to let go of the guilt.

St. Teresa of Avila went through a phase of her life when she hardly prayed at all under the guise of humility. She thought as a wicked sinner she didn't deserve to get favors from God. But turning away from prayer was like "a suckling child. If it turns away from its mother's breasts, what can be expected for it but death?"[4]

I had apologized to my daughter. I had gone to Confession. It was time to move on.

I think of my friend and her fear that she was a horrible mother because I had the sense she was giving up on herself and closing herself off to God's grace. My friend is a very savvy entrepreneur, and she suddenly started more and more projects because she felt like she was good at that but was horrid at being a mother. I told her that her children wanted her there more than she would ever know, even if she was an imperfect mother who lost her cool occasionally. She needed to forgive herself. She needed to pull each of her sweet children onto her lap and hold them closer.

BEAUTIFULLY FLAWED

When I was on bed rest with my fourth baby, I decided to pick up knitting again. I had tried it before when I was pregnant with my first. I took lessons and everything and had lovely plans to knit together a baby blanket for my firstborn. I still have a beautiful corner of said baby blanket tucked away in my closet. It might make a nice hankie someday. I gave up knitting after I made that blankie corner and made a few shoddy scarves where all I noticed were the mistakes.

This time around, my perspective had shifted. Every row still wasn't perfect, but I kept at it, marveling at how the varicolored scarf grew longer. I focused on progress, not perfection, and was surprisingly happy watching the rows increase. I accepted a few loose stitches instead of just letting the whole thing unravel.

God wants you and I to do the same. Accept yourself and all of your faults, quirks, and loose stitches. Turn to him with your prayers. And never give up if your prayer life isn't the way you think it ought to be. Have trouble focusing on the Word? Join the Distracted Mom Club. Wake up early to spend time with God and end up spending time with a little lark who sprang out of bed the moment you sat down with your cup of tea? Me too. Prayer, like mothering, doesn't have to be perfect to be meaningful. Sometimes just showing up is enough.

In your prayers, ask for grace, but also start to think more about others rather than being so focused on yourself. We will never feel better about ourselves by becoming more and more consumed by ourselves.

I'm not suggesting that as mothers we have no power to change or shouldn't even bother trying. I'm not condoning any angry outbursts directed at these impressionable souls entrusted to us. Yes, let's work on changing our undesirable behaviors, work on our prayer habits and how we react to the joys and sorrows in life. But, remember: there's a big difference between striving for excellence and trying to be perfect. Our God is a loving God who never wants us to settle for less than our worth, to give up trying, or to bury our mistakes beneath a veneer of perfection. But he is also a God who wants us to need him. He invites you to surrender everything to him and to offer your threadbare self so that he might help knit you back together so that you can become whole, if not beautifully flawed.

Our heavenly Father came to be the great physician to heal the sick (see Mt 9:10–13). He draws us close to him so he can heal us because we are sick and broken—not because we are well.

Dear Mama, you are a prized child of God. But please remember this, too: you are human. You cannot expect to look perfect, be a perfect wife or mother, eat perfectly, or *be* perfect. When you stumble, pick yourself up, even if you have to do it again and again. God doesn't pay attention to the falling. He's watching the rising. What will we do with ourselves, our lives, and our brokenness?

WILL JUDAS PLEASE STAND UP?

Several years ago, I was reading a story to my children called *The Road to Easter*. When we got to the bit about Judas sneaking away during the Last Supper, Madeline announced that she had once played the part of Judas in a skit during her First Communion prep at church. "No one else wanted to be him," she said.

"Why?" her little sister asked.

"Well," I explained, "probably because Judas hurt Jesus."

"But it was just pretend," Madeline added.

"Of course," I agreed, smiling.

I've often thought about poor Judas, the betrayer of Christ. Madeline was right: no one wants to be Judas. At first look, it's because, as I explained to my kids, we don't want to be the one who hurts Jesus, the person whose betrayal leads to the scourging and nails driven into his hands and feet.

I've never been convinced, however, that Judas's kiss of betrayal was his worst offense. We all betray Jesus. This happens every time I hurt a family member or choose not to show compassion to a fellow human being, including the wakeful child who asks for "one more cup of water, please," and I screech, "You know where the faucet is!"

It's interesting, too, that Peter, who openly denies any allegiance to Christ—not once but three times—even after pledging his undying love to him at the Last Supper, is the guy we all admire, the part we all want to play. Jesus chose Peter to be the rock of the Church. "You are Peter, and upon this rock I will build my church" (Mt 16:18), proof that Jesus forgives and uses weak people to build his Church.

So what's the difference between the hero and the disciple who will go down in all of history to be the villain no one wants a part of?

Judas's gravest sin was not his betrayal; it was his complete and utter despair. Peter accepted his weakness and humbled himself before Christ. Peter believed in God's mercy. Judas did not.

Madeline was only playing pretend when she took on Judas's role. Sometimes I'm not. There have been several particularly dark chapters in my life when I have felt too unworthy to bring my needs to God. Back in my twenties, I went to Confession for the same exact sin over and over, and I never felt washed clean. Guilt about something you did is one thing, but shame comes into play when you feel badly about who you are. In the throes of depression, I have felt nothing but despair. I have felt as if I'd betrayed my God-given vocation as a mother and there was no way out. I was Judas hanging from the tree. I'd put the noose around my neck. I'd condemned myself. God was the one who gently called me back with his mercy and his unwavering love.

Who will you be as a mother? And I don't mean who you'll be to the outside world who might think you've got it all together, but who will you be in your heart? Will you be Judas—so mired in despair and afraid of your imperfections that you hide from Christ? Or will you be Peter—the rock whose courage was often reduced to the size of a pebble?

Give your fears of failure, your flaws—give it all to Christ. Put them at the foot of the Cross, and watch how he lovingly gazes down at you.

Look at your children, too. They are wellsprings of mercy. When you lose your temper or commit some other maternal misstep, don't be afraid to look into their eyes and ask for their forgiveness. Sometimes what I think are my worst mothering moments transform into beautiful lessons in love and mercy for both my children and me.

I have often shared these simple but profound words with my children when they have been upset about something they did: "There is nothing you can do that will ever take away my love for you, and there's nothing you can do to earn that love either."

Imagine how touched I was—okay, so maybe I started to sob tears and choke on my own spit bubbles—when a daughter patted my arm after I apologized for being a frazzled, snappy stress ball, and she said those very same words to me: "Mommy, there's nothing you can do that will ever take away my love for you, and there's nothing you can do to earn my love either."

Now imagine for a moment how much God loves us. There's nothing you can do to take away or to earn his love. It's there for the taking.

Mom's Time-Out

Lord, I am so far from perfect, and I will never be enough without you in my life. Like the psalmist, "I have seen the limits of all perfection" (Ps 119:96) and how it robs me of joy and keeps me from turning to you for grace and help. The deepest desire of my heart is to love and serve you with my words, with my actions, with my role as a wife and mom, and with my entire life, but this can be so hard. Oh, how I need you! Please, sweet Jesus, help me to never stop trying

to be and give my best. But please also help me to
remember that no matter how badly I fall short, your
love and mercy is here for me and your light shines
brilliantly through my own brokenness. Amen.

Write down five things you're really good at as a wife, mother, friend, and/or disciple of Christ. If you have trouble thinking of five things, ask someone who loves and knows you well what your strengths are or what you excel at. Give thanks for these gifts.

CHAPTER 4

Let the Mothering Games Begin!

MOTHERHOOD IS NOT A COMPETITION

EVIL EARWORM

I will be better than that mom over there. In fact, I will be the *best* Catholic mom ever born into existence, and I will homeschool seventeen children, never lose my patience, and only feed them homemade, gluten-free power bars for snacks. I'll also run marathons and be a Nobel Laureate.

UNVARNISHED TRUTH

Get off your high horse. Motherhood is not a competition.

Long ago, I met a mom whose children were all blissfully sleeping through the night by eight weeks. Meanwhile, my own little
bundle of joy was a total insomniac and after eighteen months
of waking up throughout the night, I'd morphed into what I
referred to as a "mombie."

When the mom heard how wakeful my child was, she questioned my nighttime parenting. As she shared unsolicited advice
on what I should and shouldn't do to raise a good sleeper, I
started to wonder if she was right. *What if my daughter's atrocious
sleep habits really were completely my doing? Maybe my nursing on
demand had created a nocturnal boob vampire.*

But as she continued to drone on about her angel's perfect
sleep habits, my insecurity was replaced with anger. I put on my
best saccharine smile while inside I was starting to seethe as ugly
thoughts bubbled within me. *Maybe this mom's baby sleeps more
than mine because she's just not as brilliantly inquisitive. Or maybe
this mom just isn't as attentive as I am. So there.*

Every time that mother and I interacted from that point on,
I watched her carefully and secretly celebrated anything I saw
as a maternal misstep. Once her daughter pushed my own child
over, and I couldn't help but feel smug. *So maybe her child is a good
sleeper, but she's also a bully.* I had no way of knowing that one day
I would give birth to a little boy we would nickname Todzilla
because he was incredibly skilled at pushing down block towers
as well as sisters.

Sadly, I unfairly harbored disdain for this poor woman.
Maybe she shouldn't have been so tenacious about sharing her
sleep tips with me when all I needed was someone to listen to me
and remind me that *this too shall pass.* But I certainly had no right
to think less than charitable thoughts about her, her mothering,
or her clinophile of a child either.

Chances are, at some point, most of us will find ourselves
envious or maybe just wary of another mom. Maybe we've justi-
fiably felt threatened by another mom's comments or judgments
about our parenting. I doubt that most mothers are mean-spirited

people with derisive zingers always at the tip of their tongues. When we passionately share what has worked for us or lash out at moms who do things differently than we do, we're simply looking to validate our own choices. I know that's what I was doing when I secretly accused my friend of being an inattentive nighttime parent. I was anxious that maybe I was doing something wrong and my baby wasn't sleeping because of the parenting choices I'd made.

When I gave birth to baby number two who did—cue the choirs of angels—sleep through the night curled up next to me without needing constant nosh sessions, I realized my oldest was just programmed not to need as much sleep. Our sleepless nights had more to do with her nature than my nurture, but I didn't know that at the time, and I was seeking affirmation— not advice—that everything was going to be okay and my child would eventually stay horizontal for longer than a one-hour stretch. And that child, who is now twelve, has been known to hit the snooze button and sleep late on the weekends. Dear moms of little insomniacs, there *is* hope!

An unfortunate vehicle for expressing our subterranean fears and anxieties is pure cattiness. Women can sometimes just be a bunch of jerks. We need one another so much, and yet we're quick to judge one another and "tsk, tsk" everything from the way a peer mom's bum looks in her yoga pants to the way our neighbor disciplines her kids. The comparing, criticizing, judging, and constant assessing begins from the moment we conceive. If not us, then the media criticizes the moms who gain too much weight during pregnancy as well as those who don't gain enough. You're damned if you do and damned if you don't. Later on, moms are tempted to compete for the Mothering of the Year Award in other ways by: how we feed our families or don't, our educational choices for our children, whether our bed is shared with little and sometimes big kids or only with our spouse, our kids' reading levels, how well they dance or play sports or the cello, our kids' college acceptance letters, and so on.

Since when did mothering become a competitive sport?

Dear mothers, it's time to put an end to the mothering games. It's exhausting, depressing, and completely unnecessary.

It's time to stop feeling inadequate about our own mothering—so much so that we're tempted to blow out another mom's candle to make ours brighter. Live authentically, and other moms will be drawn to you no matter what parenting books are on your shelf. It's time that, as a sorority of mothers, we work to ensure every mother has access to support and a nonjudgmental community. It's time to call a truce to all of the different kinds of mommy wars that seem to wage online and in real life. Mainstream media loves conflict. So does Satan. He wants us divided instead of united because there's nothing with more powerful potential to bring good into the world than a closed circle of women. We will have so much more to offer our families and society beyond if we focus on what unites us. When it comes right down to it, whatever parenting choices we make, we're mothers first, and what we all have in common is that we have children we love—children we're trying to raise the absolutely best ways we know how. We just have different ways of bringing that love to life in our homes and in our hearts.

None of us is an expert at this. Maybe the mom who is lamenting about mealtime mayhem at her house just needs a hug and empathy, not a ten-step plan on how to get her picky eater to eat spinach. The moment we think we've figured this whole mothering thing out is the moment we need to cut ourselves a whopping slice of humble pie, eat it, and not try to exercise it off, either.

WHEN YOU COMPARE, NO ONE WINS

Are you ready, dear sister in Christ, to join me in what my nerdy-by-nature brain refers to as *Momraderie*?

The very first step is to stop comparing and coveting.

So many mothers compare themselves to some matchless mom they encounter in their daily lives or on Instagram. We notice the mom who sews, makes homemade meals, and runs half marathons in her spare time while we're just hoping to check "shower" off of our to-do lists. Whenever we compare ourselves to another mom, we're not doing ourselves—or them—any favors. As my friend Rachel Balducci once pointed out, when we compare, no one wins. Comparing might leave us feeling inadequate because, clearly, we're a monumental failure when compared to others.

Then again, maybe we're tempted to start feeling all high and mighty. There you are on the verge of joining your child in a meltdown in the produce aisle when you see a mom whose panty lines are showing through her translucent leggings plugging her wailing child's mouth with a big, sugar-laden, artificially colored lollipop, and you're feeling like your mothering isn't so subpar after all as you unwrap your wholesome, organic granola bar. Maybe you shouldn't be patting yourself on the back. Instead, what you might want to do is reflect upon the fact that we're all in this together, give that poor mom a reassuring smile, and ask her where she bought those miracle lollipops since her toddler is silently and happily licking one now.

When we compare ourselves to others, we can easily become lawyers and judges even though we're called to be witnesses to Christ's love. We can be tempted to praise ourselves and rely on a false sense of humility because we can always find something wrong with someone else. If your internal scripts are incessantly critical of others—or yourself—it's time to make room for grace. "By the grace of God I am what I am, and his grace to me has not been ineffective" (1 Cor 15:10). Be secure in who you are—even if you're different from every other mom you know—and give other moms permission to be who they're called to be. Women who live off grace have more grace to offer to others.

When we compare, we can also be tempted to think the grass is always greener on the other side. It's a blessing to have

mothers in our lives whom we admire, but be careful not to let
your admiration transform into full-blown jealousy. "You shall
not covet your neighbor's house" (Ex 20:17), no matter how clean
and peaceful it is.

Have you ever considered why you think the grass is
greener on that mom's side of the fence? Perhaps you know of a
homeschooling mom whose days always seem to go smoothly.
Maybe ask yourself why. Is it because her children are perfect,
studious prodigies? I doubt it. Her seamless routine might be the
fruit of hard work and organization.

Or consider the mom who fits into her pre-baby jeans. Before
you start to hate her (I know it's tough not to), consider that
maybe she works really hard at squeezing fitness into her life.
This isn't to say that you don't, but perhaps you can shift your
energy from simmering at Miss Polly Perfect into productive,
healthy changes.

At the end of the day, God is never going to help you become
someone else. He wants you to be *you*. He doesn't want you
to use other moms as your benchmark. Scratch beneath their
Instagram surface, and there's humanity there. In this sense, the
Cross is a great equalizer. Jesus died for the very ones we judge,
compete with, or covet.

My friend Bridget hates it when people call her a supermom.
She enjoys crafting and is very talented and likes to share her
creations and the homeschooling projects she does with her four
children on social media, although she also likes to share the
not-so-lovely moments. But she wishes all moms would know
that she's not good at everything, and that's okay. She's not only
embraced her strengths; she's embraced her weaknesses, too. "I
used to have mothering idols," Bridget told me:

> Like many new moms, I had a list of ladies I wanted
> to emulate. You know the ones, right? The ones who
> always have it together. The ones who never forget
> snacks when they go out. The ones who remember to

make sure the diaper bag actually has diapers in it. I wanted to be like that, but it just wasn't me. With a brain that's always on the go, I tend to forget things and rush out the door. This is not something new for me. I've always been a little scatter brained, and when I became a mom, it wasn't like I magically turned into this person I thought I'd be—or rather the person I thought I wanted to be. I imagined that motherhood would force me to finally get it together. Guess what? It didn't. To this day, four children and eleven years into this mothering gig, I still forget things and rush out the door. When I pack bags for the children to go visit their grandparents, I'm notorious for leaving out underpants. I rarely, if ever, have it all together. But it's okay. I'm okay. We're okay.

When I look back and think about the day we drove an hour away to go shopping and then two of my four children had blowout diapers only for me to discover I'd forgotten to refill the diaper bag, I just laugh. The store had diapers and wipes. I even found clearance t-shirts for a dollar each that they could wear home. If there's one thing I've learned in this wild and crazy journey, it's that very few things can't be fixed or undone.

I recently had a young mother ask me how I did it all. My answer was easy: expect bumps in the road, give yourself room to make mistakes, and remember that grace isn't something you only show to others.

ERR ON THE SIDE OF GENEROSITY

I've got some wise friends. I also have a very wise faith. The Church reveals that there's a reason we all have different strengths and weaknesses—because we're all a part of the broken but beautiful Body of Christ. A dear friend of my parents and their church's pastor, Fr. Frank Richardson, once pointed out during a homily that none of us believes it all or believes all of the time. Then he shared a story of a woman who had lost her son in an automobile accident. In her despair, she turned her back on her faith and questioned how an all-loving God could take her son in such a tragic, horrific way, especially since she had been so faithful. Fr. Frank said we could react to her fallen faith in three ways. We could say she no longer belongs in church since she'd given up on God—clearly, an unchristian and harsh way of responding to her sorrow. We could tell her she was facing only a temporary bout of depression and that everything would be fine. But this response wasn't appropriate either. Everything would not be fine—at least not for a long time. She had lost a child and would never be the same because of this great loss. Lastly, we could reach out to her, minister to her, and give her permission to grieve and to be angry. And in the absence of faith, we could believe for her.

We could believe for her.

As a community of believers, we can believe when others cannot. The Communion of Saints is at our disposal to replace our doubts with faith. Like a choir, Fr. Frank said, together we can create beautiful music even if as individuals, it's impossible to hit every note every time. Thankfully, God did not design us to be soloists. When we get off-key, we have backup singers to keep the song in harmony.

1 Corinthians 12:21–22 reminds us that "the eye cannot say to the hand, 'I do not need you,' nor again the head to the feet, 'I do not need you.' Indeed, the parts of the body that seem to be weaker are all the more necessary."

We not only need one another during bouts of spiritual dryness, we need one another every single day in the trenches of motherhood. The Body of Christ is meant to be interdependent. We desperately need each other's strengths—and weaknesses. We weren't meant to parent in isolation or canonize our fellow moms as the "perfect parents" who make us look pathetic. The

Catechism reiterates this: "The 'talents' are not distributed equally. These differences belong to God's plan, who wills that each receive what he needs from others, and that those endowed with particular 'talents' share the benefits with those who need them. These differences encourage and often oblige persons to practice generosity, kindness, and sharing of goods" (*CCC*, 1936–1937).

Your heavenly Father wants you to share your talents and allow others to help you in your weakness. Maybe some of that brown grass on your own hillside is there to help you to grow spiritually—or it's there to give another mom an opportunity to serve you.

Whenever I'm tempted to compare myself to someone else or to give in to feelings of inferiority, I remind myself of the wisdom of St. Thérèse of Lisieux, the "Little Flower." St. Thérèse learned early on that God had not created her to be big and bold like St. Joan of Arc, so instead she embraced the "little way" and made it her daily habit to do little things with big love. She is such an inspiration for moms. Her little way can help us to see the meaning and love behind the menial tasks of motherhood, such as high chair crud removal or playing chauffeur. St. Thérèse can also help us accept ourselves as God created us to be rather than worrying we're not more like someone else. In her autobiography, *The Story of a Soul*, she writes,

> I understood how all the flowers he has created are beautiful, how the splendor of the rose and the whiteness of the lily do not take away the perfume of the little violet or the delightful simplicity of the daisy. I understood that if all flowers wanted to be roses, nature would lose her springtime beauty, and the fields would no longer be decked out with little wild flowers. And so it is in the world of souls, Jesus' garden. He willed to create great souls comparable to lilies and roses, but he has created smaller ones and these must be content to be daisies or violets destined to give joy

to God's glances when he looks down at his feet. *Per-fection consists in doing his will, in being what he wills us to be.*[1]

St. Thérèse also said, "When one loves, one does not calculate."[2] In other words, stop keeping score. Jesus said to feed his sheep, not count them. Give love freely—even to the moms you're the most jealous of or who irk you. Don't worry about what your friend's kids are reading or how well they're doing in sports. When you're tempted to criticize, gossip, imitate, or compete, take a deep breath and tell yourself you're not going to go there—and encourage a fellow mom instead.

Ultimately, be confident in your role as your child's mother. The Bible alludes to insecurity as the fear of man and a snare (see Prv 29:25). That fear is what allows others' opinions of us to affect our values and choices when the only one we should be worried about following is Jesus. Pray for the grace to see what's best for you and your family. Try to remember that other moms can be examples to us but that we can't allow them to be our standard for good mothering or holiness. We're not made in the image of that beautiful mom we admire or our amazing mother-in-law. We're created to be molded into the image of Jesus Christ and to grow closer to his image and likeness.

In my early mothering days, I had it in my head that in order to be a faithful Catholic I had to follow some prescribed for-mula—have a certain number of children and raise them in a specific way. But then a wise spiritual director reminded me that holiness comes in many different incarnations. Just look at the varied lives of the saints. There were fishermen, princesses, musi-cians, mothers, priests, and soldiers. There's no one-size-fits-all to holiness or mothering. I've encountered amazing moms of one and moms of many, moms who send their kids to school and moms who homeschool, moms who sleep with their babies and moms who don't. What each of them has in common is that they're trying to make the most of their own natural gifts and talents and lead godly lives. They're women who look to God for guidance rather than trying to live up to some unrealistic ideal of their own making or based upon some other mother's life. They are secure in their roles as mothers and daughters of God.

In her book *The 10 Habits of Happy Mothers*, author Meg Meeker, MD, suggests that moms who have a healthy sense of their own value as mothers focus on what they do well rather than worrying about all the things they mess up. Then they have residual energy to build up others. She writes, "[Secure moms] are so comfortable with who they are that they are free to elevate others. Insecure mothers scour the territory before them to find a way to elevate themselves, primarily through making another mother look a little smaller, uglier, less informed, or even stupid."[3]

Which kind of mom do you want to be? Let's focus on building up others as well as ourselves. Keep asking the Spirit to mold you into the image of Christ. Your family and the world are waiting for your witness.

Mom's Time-Out

Dear Lord, make me a woman who doesn't have to show off, judge, or try to imitate anyone but you. Make me a confident woman secure in your love. You loved me first. That's all there is to it. I have my weaknesses, but I also have my strengths, and your power is made perfect in my weaknesses (2 Cor 12:9). Give me the freedom to be myself and to allow others that same freedom. Amen.

Think about what *you* enjoy, and do those things with your child rather than trying to be like another mom you admire. For example, if you enjoy doing crafts you find on Pinterest then by all means get crafty. But if the thought of glitter and glue sticks makes you break into hives then do something else together. They don't need a "craftastic" mom. They just want and need *you*. Today, choose something fun to do with your child that you'll both enjoy.

CHAPTER 5

Mom the Martyr

DON'T BE A MARTYR
FOR YOUR CHILDREN

EVIL EARWORM

A good Christian mother is a martyr
for her children and her family.

UNVARNISHED TRUTH

Mothers are loving servants, not
subservient martyrs.

Last year Madeline, my oldest daughter, had an exciting opportunity to serve as a water girl for the girls' varsity basketball team
of our local Catholic high school at a big playoff game. A friend
was going to take her since I had to get her sister Rachel to soccer
practice at the same time. Then the friend's daughter came down
with an awful cold. And then germs got a hold of me, and I was
in bed with a fever and stomach cramps, feeling like a Mack truck
had flattened me. Still, I was determined to figure out a way to
get my child to that game. But Rachel came down with a fever as
well, and I started to question whether the basketball team would
even want a potential petri dish as a water girl.

It pained me to tell Madeline the disappointing news. She
took it fairly well, but she walked around that evening with a
heavy heart, and a part of me wondered if I should have just
sucked it up and loaded Madeline, my feverish self, a sick daughter, and two other kids into the car for a thirty-minute schlep to
the game.

Madeline came to check on me and bemoan the injustices of
life.

"I'm so sorry, love," I told her.

"It's okay," she said. "I know it's not your fault, but do you
think I'll be able to be a water girl at another game?"

"I don't know," I said honestly.

"It's not fair," she said.

"It isn't," I told her. "I would hug you right now, but I don't
want to share my germs."

She offered a rueful smile and shuffled out of my bedroom. I
thought how sad I felt to see her happiness thwarted, but then I
considered how this wasn't really even a major disappointment.
There would very likely be far worse hurts that cut much more
deeply. For my smaller children—who, with fists furled, demand
I cut their sandwiches into triangles, not rectangles today—there's
no doubt real anguish lies ahead. But in their little microcosm, life
is a minefield of disappointments and things they can't control.

Yet it's not my job as their mother to rush headlong into the battlefield and save them from all their ills. Instead, what I'm called to do is to show my children compassion when something hurts and to love my children all day and every day (and some days more than others) with the mercy and goodness of Jesus.

What God doesn't expect of mothers is to grant our children guaranteed inoculation against angst, whether by over-sacrificing ourselves or denying the needs of others in our midst. To get Madeline to that game, I could have popped some anti-nausea meds in my mouth and coaxed a sick sibling and the two littles into our swagger wagon so she could fulfill her water girl dream, but the wagon would have lost its swagger right there along with Mom. And how would Madeline ever learn to embrace "thy will be done" when my decisions were conveying to her that "her will be done" no matter the cost to others?

As mothers, we're not called to be subservient martyrs for our families. A martyr is someone who dies for a cause—literally. Or it's someone who pines for sympathy and attention and exaggerates how terribly she is suffering. Who wants to partake in either of those things? Yet the latter is what so many mothers are doing. We've slapped on a high-gloss finish to the role of mommy, and we overemphasize the things that mothers do or *should* do for their children. There's even a temptation to "moralize" certain aspects of mothering. There's the subtle message, especially in some Christian mothering circles, that a mother of virtue *always* chooses to do *this* or *that* for her child. Mothers are exceedingly important; we're nurturing souls for Christ, building the Church, as well as serving as Christ-bearers in the world. But over-extolling motherhood and wrongly assuming a good mother annihilates herself—or the needs of others—to care for her children comes with potentially negative consequences.

OUR CHILDREN BECOME
SOLIPSISTIC NAVEL-GAZERS

Once my children's school called to inform me that my eight-year-old didn't have a lunch. "She *has* a lunch," the Wicked Witch of Mothering corrected, "but she forgot it." There's a difference. I gave my creative, absent-minded child one "get out of jail" pass but when she forgot her lunch twice in one week, I wasn't going to drop everything and rush to her rescue like a martyr mom might. Not that I reveled in the thought of the school staff thinking I was a cruel, heartless mother, but I knew she wouldn't starve after one skipped meal. This was a natural consequence for her failure to be responsible for her own things.

Now before anyone thinks it's easy for me to dole out "tough love," it's not. My mama bear instincts are strong, and I desperately want to protect my cubs and keep them happy. It's what drives me to safeguard my cherubs from everything from food additives to bogeymen. Sometimes I do waffle and make bad, but oftentimes easier, parenting choices. It's called "tough love" for a reason; it doesn't always feel good.

Aside from the disappointment our children might endure, "tough" mamas can be seen as cold and uncaring because sometimes it feels like the mom who sacrifices the most will win a prize—or at least she's seen as the mom who loves her kids far more than the rest of us. The postmodern helicopter parent, the one who swoops in to provide aid before her children even send out an SOS, is frequently lauded. Ironically, even as the pro-abortion message is like a knife cutting through today's parenting ethos with the message that children are more burdens than blessings, we're becoming more and more child-centered.

There are parents who clothe their children in designer labels and scold them for jumping in puddles or running through mud when that's what inquisitive children are designed to do. We fill them with only the healthiest foods, all neatly cut into the shapes of exotic zoo animals. We exercise them daily—even if that means two-hour soccer practices, incessant patty-caking, daily choreographed living room dance parties, and regular visits to huge rooms filled with inflatables. We're tempted to do everything for them—from clearing their dishes to completing their book reports.

And don't get me started on the kinds of birthday parties we throw our children these days. I was looking back at some snapshots from my third baby's first birthday. There were a few teeth in Mary Elizabeth's beaming grin. Her head was topped with a ridiculous, shiny cone birthday hat, and her pudgy fist was digging into a homemade, lopsided cake. Her smiling siblings were giggling at her cake-covered face, and she was slinging frosting at them. There was no petting zoo, ice sculptures, or avant-garde circus troupe. It was a joyously simple birthday celebration, and we all felt good about it that day. But one quick glance at carefully curated social media feeds, and you'd think we could do a little better for our precious children. If you enjoy throwing highly orchestrated and expensive birthday bashes, go for it. But your kids don't need it. I promise. And don't ever spend oodles of cash or time doing something just to impress the parental Joneses. Our children will be content with the birthday trappings from our own childhoods: a simple but delicious cake topped with candles, a gift or two, and loved ones singing off-key as we all make wishes for the birthday boy or girl's happiness.

Whether it's extravagant parties or meticulously mapped-out extracurricular schedules that leave us frazzled from all the logistics of getting Kid A to Point B while Kid B has to simultaneously be at Point C, we have to be careful what we're sacrificing. Sacrificing love and time are one thing, but if we're sacrificing money, our sanity, and time that would be better spent elsewhere to make our child feel loved with things or elaborate parties, it's time to return to the basics. Consider your own favorite childhood memories. I can't remember what I received as Christmas presents each year, but I do have cherished memories of visiting my grandparents in Chicago every December, playing with gaggles of cousins, and eating my aunt's homemade spritz cookies.

We live in a world that focuses a lot on the "outside cup." We work hard and harder so we can get the bigger house, nicer car, and take multiple trips to Disney World each year. We struggle to create the perfect experiences instead of helping our children learn how to navigate the imperfect world we live in. We mistakenly think giving our children the latest and greatest "things," not just our time and attention, is a measure of parental love. But a verse from the Gospel of Matthew offers an important warning: "You cleanse the outside of the cup and dish, but inside they are full of plunder and self-indulgence" (Mt 23:25).

As Catholics, we have to have an eternal worldview. We probably can't change the hyperfocus on the "outside cup" of worldly success—such as having a trim, fit figure while concurrently boasting a fat bank account—but we can change ourselves and how our children see what we value. We have to turn away from the pull of superficial, self-indulgent whims and toward God and the eternal. We don't want self-indulgent children. We want self-sacrificing ones.

Caryll Houselander, a great spiritual writer, encourages us to embrace simplicity and to "stop striving to reach a goal that means becoming something the world admires, but which is not really worthwhile. Instead, we realize the things that really do contribute to our happiness, and work for those. For example, we cease to want to be rich, successful or popular, and want instead the things that satisfy our deeper instincts: to be at home, to make things with our hands, to have time to see and wonder at the beauty of the earth, to love and to be loved."[1]

Our children could care less if we make cookies from scratch or let Pillsbury do some of the work—they only want the cookies and us. Love simply, and encourage the same for your children. Vacations don't need to meet some arbitrary ideal; being together is perfect enough. Help your children to shine the inside of their cups by doing good for others and choosing kindness because it's the right thing to do, not because they're going to earn a gold star for it.

HELP CHILDREN LEARN THE REDEMPTIVE GIFT OF SUFFERING

Like most parents, I'm sometimes tempted to take away all of my children's struggles—even if it means I suffer more or unnecessarily. Other times, it's difficult to say no when Thomas, my five-year-old, asks for another bedtime story while batting those long lashes of his or when he asks politely for a toy he's had his eye on for months.

Before I became a mom, I rolled my eyes at doting, smothering parents and resolved to be more of a *no-pain-no-gain* hardliner when I had kids. *What doesn't kill kids makes them stronger. Blah, blah, blah.*

My, how things change.

From the moment I conceived my first child, I was overwhelmed with an intense desire to protect my baby and to keep her safe. During my first pregnancy I was on a walk and—pregnant klutz that I was—I tripped on an uneven part of the sidewalk. I was headed belly first for the ground, but somehow I managed to throw my body to the side, and it was my hip that first made contact with the concrete.

Nothing was going to hurt my baby. *Nothing.*

Only now I see that things upset my babies all of the time. Sometimes it's even me who's doing the upsetting (*gasp!*) by gently but firmly saying no to their pleas. We have rainy days that should have been sunny so we could venture out to the zoo. We have dinners not followed by dessert. We have times when one child's needs cannot be met immediately because a sibling's needs take precedent at that moment. We have even had a day when I forced my child to wear a pair of shoes that were too small because she couldn't find her school shoes even though I remind her every single day to put them into her shoe basket. (We have shoe location issues in our family, clearly.) Watching her hobble to the car did make me feel a tad guilty, but that dramatic and dreamy child of mine has been a *little* better about keeping track of her shoes since then.

One day, my kids will likely face much bigger disappointments—broken hearts, rejections from colleges and employers, backstabbing friends, missed opportunities, and maybe worse.

There's no escaping it: pain is a part of the human condition. *Welcome to life, kiddos. It's full of disappointments.*

The world is chipping away at my children's innocent hearts every day. And yet, as tough as it is for a mother who is designed to love her children fiercely and deeply, I know it's not my job to shield them from all the angst of life.

Thomas Paine said, "What we obtain too cheap, we esteem too lightly." And didn't God say something very similar when he sacrificed his only Son for us so that we could have life? One drop of Christ's blood could have saved us all, yet he freely chose to shed every last bit of it. He gave what is beyond sufficient so that we might recognize the power of sacrificial love.

In Pope Benedict XVI's *Letter to Roman Educators*, he wrote, "Suffering is also part of the truth of our life. So, by seeking to shield the youngest from every difficulty and experience of suffering, we risk raising brittle and ungenerous people, despite our good intentions: indeed, the capacity for loving corresponds to the capacity for suffering and for suffering together."[2]

Yet it's not acceptable to talk about suffering or sacrifice anymore. Why struggle when there's an easier way? Why take the moral high road when there's a detour at every turn? And when parents feel guilty about working too much or staring down at their cell phones instead of really listening to their child, they wonder if they can make up for all that they lack and their mistakes as parents by giving their kids more stuff and shielding them from any brand of suffering.

Have I put my children's needs first and safeguarded them from some hardship? Of course. When they're babies, their needs and wants are one and the same. As they grow older, however, the line between what they need and want becomes more blurred, and I have to be more careful to draw the distinction between being connected and being too involved or too indulgent to their every whim. My children have to learn they're a part of a family in which everyone's needs have to be taken into account. Children, especially younger ones, unquestionably need more help, guidance, and protection than their parents, but that doesn't mean parents' needs are never a priority or that our kids' privations are the only ones that matter.

Ultimately, I want my own children to recognize that we're entitled to very little beyond God's love. I want them to work hard as well as to see the redemptive value of suffering. But that won't happen if I toss them a lifesaver at the first sign of distress, even when every ounce of my maternal being wants to do just that.

MORE POTENTIAL CONSEQUENCES IN THE WAKE OF A MARTYR MOM

The martyr mom might manifest in doing everything for everyone in the family. Or she may be the room mom who always throws Pinterest-worthy parties *and* looks down on the parents who don't while lamenting about how busy she always is. Or she's the mom who, day after day, doles out what she thinks is sacrificial love but is really her sanity. When mothers chronically and unctuously over-give, there's a sobering parade of people left in their self-eradicating wake.

There are their children, who might be afraid to be a martyr for motherhood like their own mothers, who sacrificed everything—and made sure their children knew about it. Mothers who selflessly give over and over and then have grown children who never call them, abandon their faith, or fall into selfish ways can find themselves embroiled in resentment. Motherhood can feel like a thankless job, and instead of seeking help or admitting how very draining motherhood can be, some mothers end up suffering from depression or burnout.

Yet despite breakdowns and burning resentment, many moms forge ahead and keep on giving as if their children are a splinter they can't remove. When we do this, yes, we sacrifice much, but our children may grow up thinking they were a major inconvenience, a parasite, sucking out the heart of their mother's life. One woman explained her reasons for not wanting to be a mother after a pro-life blog post I had written: "My mother made sure I understood how much of a burden I was. She'd tell me exactly how much I cost to raise and what she gave up when she got pregnant."

While I'm not going to whitewash motherhood to my children or to anyone else, I have to be careful of falling into the "woe is me" mentality too much. If I need help, I try to ask for it. I've relied more on my village of friends and families over the past few years than ever before. That's what ten weeks of bed rest during your fourth pregnancy will teach you. There's no shame in asking for help.

Martyr moms who are blessed to have a parenting partner also undermine the role of the father in the family. I had a friend who was exhausted dealing with a wakeful newborn, but every time her husband stepped in to help she shooed him away. She had this need to be in control all of the time. She selflessly poured herself into mothering, but the chronic sleep deprivation was taking its toll on her, and her husband started distancing himself from her and their baby. Finally, one day he told her he was worried not only about his exhausted, weary wife but also about his relationship with his child. "If you do everything, then how am I going to learn how to be a dad?" he asked. She realized he was right. So she started letting him change diapers, and she pumped some extra breast milk so he could occasionally help out with nighttime feedings. Both she and their baby benefited from the new arrangement.

You, dear Mother, are *very* important, but there are other people in your children's lives who also play special, significant roles. Don't fall into the trap of thinking "mother knows best" because sometimes you don't, and even if you do, you might not be able to always be the one on the front lines.

Finally, by exalting "mother" into a tireless and selfless superhuman, we run the risk of creating an unattainable standard for what it means to be a loving mother. Even the woman who appears to effortlessly juggle all the balls in the air isn't immune to the potential negative aftereffects, such as failed marriages, broken friendships, poor self-care, and hidden resentments.

A CALL TO SERVE

"No one has greater love than this, to lay down one's life for one's friends" (Jn 15:13). Just replace "one" with "mom" and "friends" with "children," and it paints an accurate picture of the kind of love a mom bears for her children. On a daily basis, moms lay down their lives for their children—not usually literally, but we do give up a lot in order to be mothers to our children. Gone are the days of marathon sweat sessions at the gym, lazy Saturday afternoons of curling up with a good book, a full night's sleep, and eating a leisurely meal instead of wolfing down food so we can tend to our kids' needs. There's always another diaper to be changed; another load of laundry to wash, dry, and fold; another spill to be soaked up; and another carpool, but all these seemingly mundane tasks are tiny sacrifices and a way to show our children we love them. Jesus says, "If anyone wishes to come after me, he must deny himself and take up his cross daily, and follow me" (Lk 9:23).

Many women are more naturally inclined to follow the way of the Cross, but Jesus' Cross isn't usually ostentatious, emblazoned with neon lights. It's simple. It's the giving of yourself in ordinary things. St. Théodore Guérin said, "What must we do to become saints? Nothing extraordinary—only that which we do every day—only do it for the love of God."[3]

There's only one right choice we need to make every day, every moment, no matter the cost. It's a choice that frees, not enslaves. We must choose to abandon ourselves to God, to give everything to him—the big and the small moments of making dinner for our families and kissing the tops of our children's heads—so that whatever situation arises, we will do what he wants us to do even when we might be tempted to do otherwise.

We don't martyr ourselves according to the cultural scripts that tell us mothers can do it all or place children or the role of motherhood on a pedestal; we give of ourselves all for the glory of God.

We don't empty ourselves so that we will be filled with praise and admiration for being such selfless, amazing mothers. We empty ourselves to fill the void with God.

This isn't the same as punishing yourself or neglecting your spiritual, physical, and emotional needs. It's about emptying yourself of *your* way and embracing Jesus' way. It's about ridding yourself of all that makes you weary and afraid. It's about loving your children without any strings attached. It's about just being present to your child. If God is love, and you are there for your children, then as mothers, you're constantly giving God to your children.

Of course, all the little decisions to give and to love that you make on any given day won't get celebrated much. No one is going to see you give a sick child breathing treatments in the middle of the night. They won't see you praying over your children or gathering your resolve to set boundaries for a wayward child. No one's going to give you a trophy for raising your children without much support or working an extra job so you can pay the bills. People aren't going to celebrate the countless meals you've prepared or the fact that your house looks like a war zone but you got on the floor and read book after book to your child.

Our culture's expectations for success and happiness are pushed so high that the simple beauty of being an ordinary, loving mother is lost and we feel inadequate if we don't give to the point of debt, nervous breakdowns, or splintered relationships.

We can't change the unrealistic expectations placed on us by the media and Pinterest—at least not overnight—but we can change how we see ourselves. We're not hired help. It's not a part of our job description, and it's not good for our family to do everything for them, especially if we hope to raise independent, self-sufficient kids. We have a choice. We can be martyrs, or we can be servants who choose to serve and love while being acutely aware of our limits.

I don't want my children to grow up with a mom who did everything for them and cared so much about the "outside of the cup" that she wasn't filling the inside with real, authentic love.

Enough is enough, dear mothers. Jesus is hungry for the humble over the fussy. Less of all that stuff that doesn't really matter means more of him.

Mom's Time-Out

Sweet Jesus, I know you want not great deeds but a great heart. But so often I find myself tempted to slap an "I'm a Martyr Mom" label across my forehead—to be seen as a the mom who gives all. Often, I give out of the fierce love I have for my children, but if I'm honest, sometimes I give because I don't want to seem like a failure, like I'm the only mom whose kids' hair isn't perfectly coiffed. I'm afraid of my children having to suffer, but there are days when I'm equally afraid of not being the mom I should be. Or the one I think I should be. I don't want to be an overcommitted, overtired, and overwhelmed mom. I want my children to see the beauty in the Cross, not just the Cross. Lord, help lead me out of feelings of guilt and inadequacy and help me to worship you more than my family and to trust in you alone rather than believe the cultural lies that a good mother can fix everything—even the lives of her children. Jesus, I trust in you. Amen.

Consider the wisdom of St. Jane Frances de Chantal: "What God, in his goodness, asks of you is not excessive zeal which has reduced you to your present condition, but a calm, peaceful usefulness, a resting near him with no special attention or action of the understanding or will except a few words of love or of faithful, simple surrender spoken softly, effortlessly without the least desire to the final consolation or satisfaction in them."[4] What is your "present condition"? Have you served your kids with "excessive zeal"? Are you on the verge of burnout or already burnt to a crisp? Make a list of everything you think you *should* do as a mother. Now reread the list, pray over it, and cross off anything that is self-imposed (or a result of societal pressure) or is something your children could do for themselves. In fact, write down at least one task you currently do for your family that you're going to teach your children how to do. Then choose one chore for yourself that you don't enjoy and do it lovingly for your family and express gratitude to them for the chance to serve them.

CHAPTER 6

I Am Mother! Hear Me Roar!

YOUR CHILD'S SUCCESS IS NOT A MEASURE OF YOU

EVIL EARWORM

My kids are my sole custody, and their happiness
is a reflection of my success as a parent.

UNVARNISHED TRUTH

You do not own your children; you are stewards
of them. They belong to God, not you, and they
are here to fulfill his will—not yours or theirs.

69

My mom and dad's kitchen is sprinkled with photographs of loved ones—some recent and others a peek into the long-ago past. There's a photo of my parents on their wedding day, where they look like kids to me. My mom's hair is long and straight and falls well past her shoulders, and my dad is sporting bushy sideburns.

There are photos of my brothers and me as little kids with chipmunk cheeks. There are vacation snapshots of us with sun-kissed skin and big smiles.

But there's one photo—as tiny as it is—that always seems to catch my eye. In the photograph, adorned in a small silver frame, my mom is holding my oldest brother, her firstborn, who was around three at the time. They are sitting together in a patch of browning grass, and the sky is a bowl of blue behind them. I like to imagine the wind that was blowing on that sparkling fall day, tousling my mom's strawberry blonde hair into the air. You can see my big brother has my mother's eyes—almond-shaped and the deepest of brown—eyes that smile right along with his mouth.

My mom's arms are drawing him in, holding him close, and they're saying, "I love you and always will."

A mother's saving embrace.

When I was still pregnant with my first child, I once took the photograph off the shelf and examined it more closely, trying to see if I had missed something, if there were any clues, any hints to what lay ahead. But there's nothing in my older brother's boyish grin that says anything about his future drug addiction, the lies, or the shame.

My mom has always kept that photograph prominently displayed in her kitchen. I told my mom I loved the photograph's innocence and its glittery gold happiness—the way the camera captured the sunlight shining on her soft hair and the way her unconditional love for her child is almost palpable.

"That's my favorite picture of us," she said. "It offers me hope."

Later, when I held my own innocent firstborn baby nestled in my arms, a miraculous vessel of dreams, I winced at my mom's hope. I'd finger my own precious photographs of me embracing my babies and worry that one day these snapshots might also convey only shreds of hope and serve as a reminder of when things were better, happier, and a mother's love was enough.

Early on in my mothering career, I lived in fear that if I made one wrong move in the parenting game, I would seal my first child's fate forever because, having grown up in a family touched by addiction, I knew what *could* happen. If I wasn't a model parent, if I didn't adhere to all the experts' advice on what good parenting was (and was not), I worried my children would turn away from me and find their solace in drugs, promiscuity, violence, or some other hole of despair.

So like any good mother, I poured myself into loving my child, meeting her every need. I spent a lot of time reading about parenting theories while pregnant, and I was determined to do what the experts said would produce happy, kind, well-adjusted children. I would be gentle but firm and forge a strong bond between my children and me with plenty of cuddling and focused attention in those early years. I would supply these swirling vortexes of need with enough love, worth, and empathy so that they would never stray from me or from the values I passed along to them.

My brand of love would be *enough* for them, and I would celebrate their unshakable happiness and confidence.

My own parents smiled supportively as they watched my on-the-job mother training. They were not ones to offer unsolicited advice, but one day I remember they gave me some wise counsel for raising kids that has always stuck with me. "Don't take credit for the good. That way you won't have to take credit for the bad either," they said, chuckling but only half kidding.

My mom and dad knew something I had yet to learn: that children can be loved, disciplined, and even slightly shaped, but the end product is not a product of our hands—or even our love.

LEARNING TO LET GO AND LET GOD

Today I have five children, and I'm slowly but surely learning that my nurturing and love are important but that I don't "own" my children, and I certainly don't own their behaviors, especially their less-than-desirable ones. I'm merely a steward of these gifts given to me. And, frankly, I have very little control over these willful creatures. I can love them all I want, but they will still run away from me; bark "No!" at me; refuse to sleep, eat, or poop; or not always say "please" and "thank you."

God did not bless me with the most easygoing children. Mine are of the spirited variety—or sparkly, as my friend described them one day when they were all vying for my attention in sweet but demanding and animated ways. My children are marked with brilliant defiance. A "why?" follows every request. Even though mothering them sometimes feeling like an Olympic sport, there are days when I feel like I did an okay job as their mom. But there are lots of other days and even weeks when I feel like a total failure, when I'm pretty sure I've royally screwed up my kids and they'll all end up in therapy. Those are the days when I'm in awe of my children's deep pools of mercy and how eager they are to love imperfect me.

There are also days when my children make me really proud. They make sacrifices for each other and perform good deeds without any expectation of getting a gold star. Then there are moments when they hit and scream and act like feral animals, and no amount of prayer or "saving embraces" from me—or from the straitjacket—can save them.

That's when I am faced with the painful truth: there is no saving embrace. At least not in our own arms.

Christian parenthood is a lot like Christian life: it demands we relinquish control. We have to release ourselves from thinking that as our children's mother, we have sole custody of them. The children we love so much are creations of God, loved by God, and belong to God. Christian motherhood requires us to accept our children for who they are and let them face the consequences of their actions. We are to serve our children but not in a way that enslaves or controls them or impairs our own ability to see God's will in our own as well as our children's lives. We offer them boundaries, but we don't keep them locked away. Jesus doesn't try to control us. Why do we try so hard to control our own children?

We can lavish them with only organic food served on BPA-free dishes while they listen to Mozart, and they still might get sick or join a heavy metal band and adorn themselves with numerous body piercings. Yes, we can pray and, of course, cling to hope, but we can't coerce or even love our children into a happy, fulfilled life. There is no such thing as an insurance policy in the realm of parenting.

In the end, our children were created to fulfill not our own will but God's. We have to be careful of making too much of ourselves and too little of God.

I'm well aware that my children will make bad decisions just as I have, but I also am beginning to grasp that while I will never give up on my children or lose hope, I may have to give them up to God. This is what my own parents had to do with my older brother. They finally realized they could not fix him or save him. His addiction was not their fault. They did their best. But so often we gauge our success as parents by the choices our kids make.

When my son started preschool, we had a tumultuous beginning. One day during pickup, he sprinted away from me and proceeded to hurl a rock off a ledge, narrowly missing a car windshield below, while other parents and their perfect cherubs looked on. I sprinted to him, captured his thrashing and preternaturally strong body, and proceeded to wrestle him into his car seat. He screamed at me, and I started to cry, wondering what was wrong with my parenting or with my beloved son. That afternoon I actually e-mailed his teacher, asking if she'd noticed any red flags for my son being a psychopath. I didn't actually use the word "psychopath," but that thought did cross my mind as I watched him gleefully throw boulders to the parking lot below. I can laugh now at my inflated worry and desperation, but at the moment I was convinced my pathetic parenting had produced a raging maniac instead of what the teacher referred to as a "very strong-willed but bright four-year-old little *boy!*"

Thomas was my first experience with an X and Y chromosome, and his use of physical strength to express everything from love (his big bear hugs are the best) to anxiety (throwing big rocks at cars isn't so nice) was new to me. Instead of accepting his natural design and working to help him express his emotions in a healthier manner, I sometimes chalked up his wildness to my abysmal parenting.

Similarly, when one of my children receives an award for Christian character, it's tempting to pump my capable mom fist in the air. There are ample moments when I'm tempted to gloat at my parental prowess: "I am Mom! Hear me roar!"

Then I catch wind of my mom and dad's advice again: *Don't you dare take credit for the good because remember all that bad stuff— the nose-picking (you didn't teach your kid to do* that, *now did you?), the craziness, the preschool boy who talks about butts and guts way too much—well, of course that has nothing to do with you, right?*

Because as much as we parents tightly hold on to this idea that we are the primary shapers of our children—that they're the puppets and we have the strings—parenting is merely an influence on children. How you nurture and raise your children is one factor of many.

We're not masters of our own fate; we certainly cannot be masters of these entirely separate and willful beings.

Here's an idea: Instead of obsessing over what parenting guru of the moment is saying is the secret to parental success and raising respectful children, why not focus more on your own obedience to God? You're only held accountable for your own obedience, not your children's.

Put God at the center of your life. Ponder his goodness more than your own and your children's weaknesses, and remember when your headstrong teen is breaking your heart or all of your kids are leaving the Church that their stories aren't finished yet. God is a sneaky author who seems to like surprising plot twists. He transforms even the worst sinners into saints. He knows what he's doing. Can you trust him? Maybe if it's not okay yet, that's because it's not the end.

Whatever parenting challenge you're facing right now, perhaps it's time you take a deep breath and let go and let God. Take solace, dear mamas, that no matter what you and your children face in this journey together, God is with you—and he believes in you even if you no longer believe in him.

For just a moment, consider how much you love your children. Now magnify that by infinity. That's where you'll find God. "As a mother comforts her child, so I will comfort you" (Is 66:13). "You are precious in my eyes and honored, and I love you" (Is 43:4).

God loves you and your children more than your limited human heart could ever grasp. And although we mean a lot to our children, we can never be anywhere close to fulfilling them in the way that God can.

Does your newborn refuse to sleep? Is your toddler biting everyone he meets like a bloodthirsty vampire? Has your older child stopped talking to you? Do you have a grown child who has abandoned her faith? Do you have a child suffering from a sickness, depression, an eating disorder, or an addiction? Release these children into God's care. Pray day after day, "Jesus, I trust in you." Yes, it's scary to stop trying to control or to "fix" your child, but it's equally liberating. It frees you from a sense of guilt and responsibility over your child's every choice and action. It allows your child to choose God for herself.

St. Monica is a beautiful example of letting go and letting God. She never gave up on her son (the now greatly revered St. Augustine) even when he was living a reckless and spiritually depraved life. She had the confidence that God was not finished with Augustine yet and that her heavenly Father would not

forsake her or her child. St. Monica found peace in the unconditional love she knew God had both for her and for her wayward
son: "While praying for Augustine's conversion, St. Monica had
a consoling dream in which an angel reassured her, 'Your son
is with you.' When she later told Augustine about the dream,
he snidely remarked that they might easily be together—if only
Monica would reject her Christian faith. Monica immediately
responded, 'He did not say that I was with you; he said you were
with me.'"[1]

Her faithful, resolute response made an impression on Augustine, and we know the end of this story. St. Augustine is now a
renowned Doctor of the Catholic Church. Who knows how our
own responses, our mercy, our hope, and our prayers might be
impacting our own children? St. Monica and her redeemed son
give every mother hope for her children and anyone who hasn't
lived an ideal Christian life.

THY WILL BE DONE

There's another mother we can learn a lot from when it comes to
obedience and trust: our Blessed Mother.

Mary didn't always understand what was going on or even
why Jesus did certain things. Think of that day she thought she
lost her son and then found him three days later praying in the
temple:

> His mother said to him, "Why have you done this to
> us?"...
>
> [Jesus replied,] "Why were you looking for me?
> Did you not know that I must be in my Father's
> house?" (Lk 2:48–49)

In other words, Jesus is saying, "Why are you worried about me?
Don't you know what I'm all about?"

Like other times in Mary's life, she doesn't completely understand what's going on, but she accepts it and puts her trust in God.

Now picture Mary at the foot of the Cross. Here is a mother in agonizing emotional pain being forced to watch her beloved son suffer—and through absolutely no fault of his own. She surely must have asked God, just as Jesus did in the Garden of Gethsemane, Why can't you take this pain away from my son and from me? But, also just like Jesus, she accepted with grace and profound faith God's will for her and for her son.

Not my will, but yours be done.

Our Lady faced insurmountable agony, yet she never lost hope. And for good reason. After Jesus' Crucifixion, on the third day, he rose again. Like Mary, we have to place our own and our children's suffering in the tomb, trust in God and the mystery of the Cross, and wait with hopeful hearts.

As mothers, we love our children deeply. We can roar, but we still may not be heard. We can sing them lullabies, but we can't make them sleep. We can parent with wisdom and grace and teach our children about faith, but they still might abandon God. We have far less control over our children than we'd like to admit. And the good that so often does bloom in our children—well, we owe all of that to the glory and grace of God.

Now when I look at the kitchen photograph of my older brother and my mom, I finally understand why she couldn't help but hold on to the hope that he would one day get better. In an act of profound trust and humility, she released her own power to save her son to her heavenly Father. I know now, too, that my mom's own maternal love is a wise, mature love that acknowledges where her responsibility to her child ends and where her responsibility to God begins.

Those sweet wounded, willful, wonderful children who sometimes drive you crazy and at other times drive you to love to the extreme will grow up and become whom they were created to be, in spite of you. You can do everything "right" (whatever the experts are saying is "right" at the moment), or you can feel like you've botched up things big time. But then, one day, you'll take a step back and see that, like a young sapling, your child has a bent all of her own. Even in the most fertile soil, things do not always grow as they should. Then again, tender, green shoots of life magically appear in even the most rocky and arid land.

Dear Mamas, don't be afraid to get dirty, to dig deep into your own heart and into those of your children, but don't be afraid to let go, either. That's where God is—in the beautiful, heart-wrenching surrender.

Mom's Time-out

St. Monica, please help me to have the trust and faith in God's love and mercy that you did. You never gave up on your son, but you did give him up to God. You never stopped praying and hoping. Help me to do the same. And while I pray that my motherly love will always be enough, if someday it's not, help me to cast any blame aside, to hold on to the faith that better things are to come, and to detach myself from thinking I can save my children. Help me to do what's best for them—even if it means losing them so that they can be found. Amen.

Do you oftentimes find you're holding yourself accountable for things you cannot control? For today, tune out your inner monologue. Be kind to yourself, accept your children as they are, and let God do his work.

CHAPTER 7

The Old Woman Who Lived in a Shoe

EMBRACE YOUR UNIQUE STAGE IN MOTHERHOOD

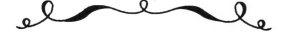

EVIL EARWORM

I thought motherhood would get easier, but it's only getting harder and lonelier. My kids are growing up. Meanwhile, I'm getting old.

UNVARNISHED TRUTH

Embrace the new seasons of motherhood.

Several years ago, thanks to my husband's new job, we relocated to a thriving college town brimming with local musicians, athletic events, and culture. Before our big move, two thoughts came to mind. First, this town would be the perfect place to raise a family. It had everything a city had to offer—minus the traffic and crime. Second, I foolishly told myself, *I'm the epitome of young and hip and am just like all those college kids. I can even rock a pair of trendy jeans if need be. Bring it.*

The good news is the town did turn out to be an ideal location for our family. But from the moment I noticed a gaggle of college girls walking in our neighborhood, all of them sporting scant athletic shorts, long sheets of straight hair, and dewy, flawless skin, I knew my second assumption about me fitting right in with twentyish saplings was delusional.

At age twenty-five, I became a mother at a fairly young age by today's standards. Still basking in the springtime of my youth and enjoying a mutant metabolism, aging seemed like something that happened to other people. Although I frequently felt tired amid the fragmented sleep and nonstop nursing, I didn't feel old. Even as our family grew and my age crept higher, I didn't fear the sands of time. I still don't, really. Aging isn't something that scares me so much as frustrates me. As a once-upon-a-time competitive runner, I used to worry about my pace. Now I worry about coordination. Recently, I tripped during a run around campus, and I fell on my head. Who breaks their fall with their head? Apparently, old ladies like me. After examining my head abrasion, my husband jokingly said I might want to consider wearing a helmet while running.

Sometimes physical limitations are tough for me to accept. I still want to do everything I was once able to do, like just stop *thinking* about eating pizza and ice cream and—*poof!*—magically lose five pounds or chase after a sprinting child and actually be able to catch him without feeling as winded as Hurricane Ian.

Also, embracing my skin's current condition isn't always a walk in the park—and certainly not a speedy sprint in the park.

Growing old gracefully would require far less effort if pimples weren't a part of the equation. Honestly, my face is defying science and capable of producing wrinkles and the zits of pubescent youth simultaneously—*amazing!*

But upon closer examination, it's not my dowdy, pimply, wrinkly, hip-popping adult status that makes me pause. What has been far more taxing on me emotionally is not my own age but my children's ages.

My children, more than the throngs of whippersnappers inhabiting my hometown, make me acutely aware of how quickly the years are passing by. Our children are walking timepieces, always marching forward, and sometimes even calling us out on how outmoded or technologically inept we are.

"What are you wearing?" tween of mine asked before a soccer game this past spring.

"New shorts. Why?"

Sure, I'm old, but I was acting as if I was in high school again, seeking the approval of a tomboy of a girl who knows and cares little of fashion.

"Well, you definitely *look* like a soccer mom," she said matter-of-factly as she pulls her long socks over her shin guards and slips into her cleats.

To be fair, I *am* a soccer mom, and we *were* off to a soccer game, but I'm not ready to be cast in one of Tina Fey's mom jeans commercials just yet.

I'm also not always ready or prepared to take a step back from my once very hands-on mothering role. Not so long ago, I had four babies under my roof and was in the business of micromanagement. I specialized in hazardous waste removal and was wiping bums of several children each day. My life back then really did seem to revolve around bowel movements and sleep. I used to joke that I felt like a celebrity because everyone wanted to sleep with me, and I had a constant entourage. But that entourage is following me around less and less these days, and I'm slipping more into a consultant role with most of my children. I'm forced to take a step back and listen more than talk, especially with my oldest, who is on the cusp of becoming a full-blown teenager. I find I must teach and guide more than control and accept the challenges of raising older children along with having little ones thrown into the mix.

The French philosopher Henri Bergson wrote, "To exist is to change, to change is to mature, to mature is to go on creating oneself endlessly."[1] This hits home as a mother. My role is no less important—and unfortunately, no less difficult—as my children grow older. It's just different, and I constantly have to adapt, accept the new seasons, and seek grace and joy in the present while not looking back or too far ahead.

THERE WILL BE POOP

While I was in the process of writing this book, I started to make peace with the size of my family and the fact that my youngest would be a five-year-old boy before these words were published. I stupidly cleared out all things "baby" from my home and decided it was time to focus on this season of motherhood and to celebrate milestones like being diaper-free. My husband and I also started to make plans for a trip out West because we have never been there and want our children to experience nature at its finest. We both agreed all four children were finally old enough to enjoy an active vacation, and we started putting a little money away each month to save for the adventure.

Then I took a pregnancy test, not really thinking I was pregnant because my cycle had been all over the place, but I just wanted to be sure—sure that my plans and acceptance were spot-on.

So much for seeing Yellowstone. I was pregnant. And old. And without any baby paraphernalia. Cue Alanis Morissette's song "Ironic." Oh, God, you do have a brilliant sense of humor, don't you?

I started to cry when I saw those two pink lines, and for the first time my tears weren't out of joy but more of the "What the heck am I going to do?" variety. Then I peed on four more sticks in case of a false positive. After I was faced with plenty more pink lines, worries flooded me at the same time as a wash of hormones took over. Those first few weeks were terribly difficult. But as God so often does, he gifted me with divine nudges that all was going to be okay. Two days after the positive test, my oldest walked into the kitchen and said out of the blue, "Can we adopt? I know you're too old to have a baby"—*Ha! I'll show her!*—"but I really, really want a baby in the house, and I could help so much!" *Your wish is my command!*

Then I broke down and cried to one of my best friends, lamenting about how I gave all my baby stuff away, and she immediately started listing all of the things she had to give to me. God would provide through his grace and through my friends.

Still, I had a lot of anxiety about how hard it was going to be to have a baby again, especially since we're so seldom home now. But then I reminded myself how every season of motherhood has been hard.

Sure, all-day pregnancy nausea is no fun. Yes, it was going to be hard to juggle a baby on top of an already jam-packed schedule. But motherhood has always been tough; yet with God's grace, I've somehow risen to the challenge. This time will be no different.

I've never seen the movie *There Will Be Blood*, but it always has sounded very dramatic. It's also made me think the title of my life story might be something like *There Will Be Poop*. There's no avoiding the poop-storms of motherhood, both literally and figuratively. We might as well embrace it and accept it.

It's easy to think of the well-worn saying to "live in the moment" only in terms of savoring life and all of its vivid but easily overlooked beauty, but we have to learn to embrace the weight of the *now* even when it's not so fun—like when you walk into a bedroom and discover that your baby dug in to a dirty diaper and decided to use poop as finger paint. This happened with my fourth, and we dubbed him with the nickname Poopcasso. Do you really want to savor *that* moment?

Or when you're faced with an unexpected pregnancy and your mind is wheeling and anxiety grips your heart.

How much can a mama take? This is authenticity—the real, raw, and sometimes-poopy version of motherhood.

You can take far more than you realize. My surprise pregnancy, like so many lessons in motherhood, made me realize I was fighting against living in the moment. I wasn't accepting the now because I was so preoccupied with dwelling on the what-ifs.

Yes, I was a quasi-old woman, but I wasn't living in a shoe, and even if I sometimes didn't know what to do, I'd get through it. So will you. There will be poop. But there will also be grace.

So many mamas worry so much about how they're going to handle something—whether it's a new baby, wrinkles, a tired body, hormonal teenagers, or an empty nest—that we lose out on what's right in front of us. We're intensely afraid of the hard seasons of motherhood, but it turns out that our fear, more than the actual difficulty of where we're at, is what really robs us of joy. We can't look back and fantasize about a different life when we should be finding grace in the moment. People have a tendency to glamorize the past, to see everything before the lonely and difficult time that is *now* through rose-colored glasses.

The fear of thinking there will be more poop, less sleep, loneliness, no phone calls or texts from older children, heartache, and suffering can break a person. I think of my mom, who suffers from atypical trigeminal neuralgia, which has been labeled the "suicide disease" because a significant number of sufferers actually try to end their lives rather than deal with the intense, burning, and chronic pain. How can my mom go on like this? We don't know. We can't look ahead. She's told me she can't think about how she will live with this kind of pain for the rest of her life. She just has to embrace each day as it comes and accept her pain—as well as welcome and savor her joys—one day at a time. She cannot fear what lies ahead. None of us can.

In Fr. Jacques Philippe's *Interior Freedom*, he writes, "What really hurts is not so much suffering itself as the fear of suffering."[2]

We can't live in fear of what the next season may bring. Nor can we bank on what Tal Ben-Shahar calls the "arrival fallacy" in his book *Happier*.³ This is the belief that when you arrive at a certain destination, you'll be happy. *Once my toddler is potty-trained . . . once my high school student gets into the college of her (my) dreams . . . once I lose ten pounds . . . then I'll finally be happy.*

But the truth is, the allure of what's to come is almost always better than the reality.

When I used to be out in public with four children under the age of seven, people would often tell me it would get easier. That hasn't been my experience. It's still hard—just a different kind of hard.

My friend, Catholic blogger Michelle Reitemeyer, has seven children and would agree. When asked which stage of parenting has been the hardest, this is what she said:

> This one. And I would have answered the same way every single day for the last eighteen years, since it was eighteen years ago that I was pregnant with my oldest. There may have been easy days in there somewhere, but I don't remember them.
>
> While it's true that mothering young children can be physically draining (due to sleep issues, breast-feeding, cleaning, and carrying the child), other issues just replace those when the children grow older. Older-child challenges can be equally or even more difficult. It was wonderful when I could send all the kids off to bed at seven o'clock, but now my three-year-old doesn't go to sleep until nine o'clock most nights because our household runs on a later schedule with big-kid activities running well past eight o'clock.
>
> And I don't see things getting any easier. I have friends whose children don't practice the faith, some whose children are living with their significant others, and some whose children are having babies out

of wedlock. I think about the stresses my siblings and I have caused our parents as adults. It doesn't end; it just changes.

But parenting, like life, is not about seeking and finding an easy path or an easy stage. The key to any stage is finding joy. Some days, this is much harder than others.

I didn't want to go camping recently. The weather was supposed to be cold, and camping is a lot of work. We were driving out, and the radio stations were sparse, so we decided to put on the only CD I had in the car: Johnny Cash. Agreeing on a musician is tough in my house. The girls like Taylor Swift; the boys like Queen. But everybody likes Johnny Cash. And although most of my kids, like my husband, are not fond of singing, there we all were, belting out his tunes together. Everybody was happy; everybody was at peace. It was a moment of complete joy, of being full to the brim with God's gift of love through this marvelous thing called family. I have to remind myself, when life is hardest, when the furrows in my brow grow deeper and it hurts to smile because those muscles have forgotten how, that I need to find the joy. It is there, and if I can't see it, it is because I am allowing the to-do list, the work, to get in the way. This "stuff" is important; the work is hard, but it is all made bearable when we have joy.

Yes, motherhood is tough in all its glorious seasons, but I've found that if, as my wise friend Michelle encourages, I just accept this rather than fight it or worry over it, I'm far more open to catching ephemeral flashes of pure joy. These are the moments when I experience feelings of contentment that transcend my ordinary surroundings. There are days when a child dramatically recounts a book she's just finished as I tackle the dirty dishes.

There are handmade cards gifted to me. There's a child curled beside me as I write, content just being in my presence. I've witnessed forgiveness and reconciliation in the wake of irrational tantrums from both my children and me. These are the important details of my life story that can get overlooked if I'm too busy looking in the other direction or worrying about what may come.

Instead of wishing away the less-than-ideal moments, fearing the future, and living in anticipation of when things get better and easier, we have to accept life as it is and look for the little joys that are all around us in Johnny Cash songs and in a child's spontaneous hug. We can't dream of a cleaner, wrinkle-free, brighter, less stinky, less painful life. We have to accept the now, live in it, and learn from it.

OF ALL THINGS VISIBLE AND INVISIBLE

You also have to accept that as a mother, you always have a great purpose. Feeling purposeless is a barrier to joy, so you may need to remind yourself of a few essential truths. First, why we are here transcends making sure dinner is on the table every night. We are called to communion with God. We will only find truth and happiness in him. "Only in God will [you] find the truth and happiness [you] never [stop] searching for" (*CCC*, 27). Being a good, happy mother might be the target, but God is the bull's-eye. Always keep your aim on him.

Second, your work as a mother—whether obvious or not—has meaning. My mom has grown children and wears a grandmother hat now, but she says she's still very much in the game as a consultant and sometimes just as a prayer warrior way off on the sidelines. She's still punching in her mom time card every single day.

I know there are moms who dread the baby stage, but I relish it because I feel so purposeful. My babies need me to survive. Likewise, infants, while certainly physically exhausting, are beautifully simple to me. I nurse them when they cry, and they're at least briefly satisfied. They want only mama. They need only my arms to be comforted. My babies' first smiles were big returns for my investment. I likewise have an excuse to "do nothing" except care for my baby. People allow you that when you have a newborn, but when you have older kids, it feels like more is expected of you—things like being manager for the soccer team or making homemade snacks for the kids to share with friends. And when you have both older and younger children, you just feel overleveraged, all over the place, and like there's not possibly enough of you to go around.

My purpose seems a little more muddied these days. As children grow older, even if a new baby is added to your family, it's easy to feel more like a glorified waitress or taxi driver. The fruit of our work doesn't seem to be ripening all that much because raising a child into adulthood is a long, laborious process. As children grow older, we become more hidden. And so does our work.

When my preschooler was around two, he delicately cupped my chin in his dimpled hands, widened his bright, brown eyes, and said to me, "Do laundry. Make dinner."

I have to be honest here: in that tender moment, I was expecting him to profess his unfettered love to me, not give me a to-do list.

I chuckled and smiled at him, but my heart felt an ounce or two heavier.

As my children have grown older, I sometimes feel like my life has been reduced to a list of menial tasks. I clean. I nag. I schlep kids around town. I listen to arguments about why my oldest should be able to have a social media account of some nature, and I still always end up saying no. I'm simply the person who cleans up spills, folds clothes, and makes sure permission slips are signed and returned to school. I feel like people rarely notice all that I do. There are days when I feel taken for granted, used, and ignored.

A good mom-friend of mine once asked me if I ever feel invisible. *Um, yeah. All of the time.*

Being a mom, especially when there are no physical signs such as a pregnancy bump, leaky breasts, or simply a little child in your arms, deals far more with that which is invisible. Love cannot be quantified, counted, or priced. It can only be given. Sometimes it's given in more obvious ways such as when you hold a tired child. Sometimes it's doled out in meal after meal you serve day after day. Sometimes love is offered in a "No, you can't have an iPod touch even if every other almost-nine-year-old in the world has one." When you give that kind of love, you're only given rejection and anger in return. Your work is unyielding. It's tireless. It brings joy, but it hurts a lot, too. There's nothing extravagant about it. I'm not building skyscrapers. I'm not piecing together perfect prose. I'm not saving lives as my husband does on an almost daily basis, reading mammograms and catching cancer in its earliest forms. There are occasional love notes and handpicked flowers (thank God for those gifts of gratitude), but there are no raises, promotions, or great accolades, and I'll certainly never be up for a Pulitzer Prize, Grammy, or even finish first in a race. No podium climbing for me, but there's another ascending, a drawing closer to love itself. Motherhood is surely a path to sanctity, especially if we give our work—even the most tedious tasks—a greater purpose.

I personally struggle with this dying to self and all the quiet, unnoticed labor that is a part of the current season of mothering I've found myself in. At some point in our mothering lives, most of us will look at the nature of our work and see it as mundane or even useless. But "as the Jewish philosopher Martin Buber wisely stated, 'It is not the nature of our work, but its consecration that is the vital thing.'"[4]

However old we feel and whatever stage of motherhood we find ourselves in, all that we have and all that we do, the visible and the invisible—from the counter-wiping to the limit-setting— is not only for our families but for the greater glory as well.

Mom's Time-Out

Dear God, please help me to find the grace of this season. Allow me to trust in your providence and goodness and that you have great plans in mind for me—"plans for [my] welfare and not for woe, so as to give [me] a future of hope" (Jer 29:11). Replace my fears and doubts with trust and faith. Remind me to enjoy my time with children, whatever their ages, but to also recognize when it's time to let go and not to hold them so close they can't be their own people. My children are growing older every day. So am I. But I need an eternal worldview. In all my days and through-out all my ages, I long to serve you, to seek joy in the now, and when necessary, to suffer with courage and grace. I love you, my Father, above all things. Amen.

Read Ecclesiastes 3:1–15. Reflect upon all of the different seasons and "appointed times" in life. What season do you find yourself in currently? What are the joys as well as challenges you're facing? What can you do to better trust that "God has made everything appropriate to its time, but has put the timeless into their hearts so they cannot find out, from beginning to end, the work which God has done" (Eccl 3:11) as well as to recognize "that there is nothing better than to rejoice and to do well during life. . . . All can eat and drink and enjoy the good of all their toil—this is a gift of God" (Eccl 3:12–13)? The next time you find yourself in a mothering poop-storm, remind yourself of another hard period you went through and the fact that you survived and even perhaps even learned from the experience.

CHAPTER 8

When There's no Joy in Mothering or in Life

BEING A MOM IS HARD, BUT YOU DON'T HAVE TO DO IT ALONE

EVIL EARWORM

I am tired, sad, and lonely—and I deserve to be all of these things. If I was stronger, better, or prayed more, I wouldn't feel this way. Parenting isn't supposed to be this difficult.

UNVARNISHED TRUTH

Feeling this way is not your fault, and newsflash, if motherhood is a path to sanctification then it's not going to be easy.

It was a beautiful fall day. A brilliantly blue sky provided a breathtaking backdrop for a canopy of leaves dusted in gold. I pulled my minivan into our driveway, opened the automatic doors, and handed my oldest the keys to the house. The kids filed out of the van, bouncing with an unflinching optimism that made me wince. My mood was in stark contrast to both the perfect day and my little, wide-eyed optimists.

I sat alone in silence long after my children, the loves of my life, had vanished inside the house. As I sat there, immobile and wondering what was the point of all of this—life, feeling lonely and sad despite my abundant blessings—a storm of sadness grew progressively stronger within me. I tried praying. I tried taking deep, renewing breaths. In fact, I'd tried all of this a lot lately. I desperately attempted to envision myself in a happier, more peaceful place, but that content woman I saw in my mind was only a ghost of the person I was in that instant. That joyful, hopeful woman was dead to me. And so I began to weep, my tears a window into my broken heart.

My crying wasn't only entrenched in sadness; it was stemming from an intense self-loathing. I hated myself because of what I perceived as a personal defect—my inability to be happy, to not be anxious, to be able to handle a simple, blessed life of caring for my healthy, fun kids. *What's wrong with me? There are people who are really suffering. Why am I so overwhelmed and sad? Why can't I just get a grip? Why am I so weak, so faithless?*

In that dark pocket of time, I hated myself so much that I honestly thought the family I loved so fiercely deserved much better than this flawed, screwed-up woman. *They'd be happier without a messed-up mom,* I told myself. *What's the point?* ran through my mind over and over like a crazed ticker tape.

Remembering how I felt and the irrational thoughts I had still terrifies me. That awful day was almost four years ago, and until sharing this, only my husband and a few friends who were there for me one night—when the emotional floodgates unexpectedly flew open and I poured my heart out—knew about these desperate, tragic thoughts.

That day the glossy patina that had been my finish for so much of my life peeled away, and while my beloved children waited for me to join them inside our beautiful, safe home, I sat alone and fantasized about ending it all. But something—a shred of hope inside of me—forced me to call my husband instead. He can't always answer his phone at work, but on this day he did.

And grace took over. Even today I can feel that grace, and it brings grateful tears to my eyes.

"I need help," I choked out before the wracking sobs took hold of me.

On the other line, there was no judgment, shaming, or admonishments to "pull yourself together." There was only unconditional love. My husband told me to go inside and sit tight, and he made phone calls and helped me to help myself.

Today, at this moment, I pray that I might be able to help another lonely mother out there who is reading these raw, difficult-to-write, and honest words. Not all moms will suffer from soul-crushing depression, anxiety, addictions, eating disorders, abusive relationships, or other heavy hardships. But all moms suffer. Once you become a mother, it's inevitable.

MOTHER, QUEEN OF SORROWS

Whenever mothering hurts—whether physically or emotionally—my thoughts drift to Mary. I don't only see her just at the foot of the Cross. Instead, I consider all of the sorrows she endured. The Church identifies seven to be exact: the prophecy of Simeon; the flight into Egypt; the loss of the child Jesus in the temple; the meeting of Jesus and Mary on the way of the Cross; the Crucifixion; the taking down of the Body of Jesus from the Cross; and the burial of Jesus.

Mary's heartache began at the presentation of Jesus in the temple (see Lk 2:22–40). As Mary and Joseph offer their son to the service of God, their hearts are filled with joy. But in an instant, Mary's happiness is lost in sadness as Simeon foretells the pain for herself, her son, and his followers.

The presentation—like each of our own journeys into motherhood—reveals the inextricable double helix of love and heartache that comes with being a mother. Mary knows that she and her son are going to suffer. And so will we.

There will sometimes be no joy—or very little of it—in motherhood or in life. If you find yourself in a joyless place, this doesn't make you weak or a bad mother. This doesn't make you any less a Christian than other mothers you admire. You can be strong. You can be faithful. You can love your children with all your heart, and you will still sometimes feel as if you are shrouded in darkness, unable to see the light.

So what do you do during these dark moments—or days or years? First, realize you're not alone.

EVERYBODY HURTS

For as long as I can remember, I've suffered from bouts of melancholy and anxiety. I started keeping a diary as soon as I could first fashion letters into words, and even the earliest entries are marbled with gloomy thoughts. In other entries, you can almost feel the forced optimism, the effort it took for me to see the silver lining or the woefully empty cup as being half full. My journals during my young adult years read more like Sylvia Plath than what you might expect from my sunshiny Pollyanna exterior.

I didn't know I was depressed. The gripping sadness that seemed to come from nowhere shamed me. I reserved it for my journals, and when I did share my vulnerability, it was frequently met with indifference. I had a college boyfriend (who turned out not to be very nice) who called me crazy, and I believed his words to be true for a long time. *Something was wrong with me. If I tried harder, prayed more, stopped my selfish navel-gazing, I'd be like everyone else—grateful, happy, normal.*

It was motherhood—even more than suffering from and overcoming a clinical eating disorder—that really helped me to finally accept and even embrace my cross. Yes, I was born a little broken, but what I was trying to do—to put forth a superhuman effort day after day to never lose my patience with my energetic, spirited children, to be perfect, and to be an incessantly joyful mother and person—wouldn't be easy for anyone, let alone someone who truly struggled with clinical depression.

In our joy-filled, Catholic, first-world, blessed bubble where Christ is at the center of our contentment and food is in no shortage, it often doesn't feel acceptable to talk about sadness, anxiety, or the fact that life can be painfully difficult. What's more, admitting that motherhood—something that is supposed to bring us joy and fulfillment—is sometimes heart-wrenching can be even more taboo. There is tremendous pressure for Christian moms to be perpetually joyful, and when you don't feel that way, there's the understated but very real message that it's your fault for not being a better Christian or a stronger person.

Since we rightfully see children and motherhood as sublime blessings, we Christian moms are deathly afraid of admitting that we sometimes feel lost, sad, desperate, anxious, and overwhelmed.

But just like Michael Stipe of R.E.M. croons, "Everybody hurts sometimes." It's no big surprise that this song is one of my Eeyore-self's favorites. Yes, everybody hurts sometimes—even mothers with lovely children.

Recently, I pulled a ligament in my thumb and had to wear a brace. People were always asking me what happened, and I'd jokingly say I was cliff-rappelling, only to admit that I was simply trying to retrieve a boneless child from the ground. A nursling of mine once scratched my eye with her paper-thin yet razor-sharp fingernail, and I had to wear a patch à la Redbeard until the corneal abrasion healed. I've suffered from mastitis and a busted, bloody nose after an amped-up toddler jolted up when I was leaning over her and her exceptionally hard head whopped me on the nose. Parenting can physically hurt us—any woman who has gone through labor knows this.

But it's perhaps the emotional wounds that leave us aching and reeling for control and strength the most.

Maybe you have a newborn whose frequent and inconsolable crying jags have left you completely wasted and depleted. Or you're the mother of a willful child who once cuddled close to you and now flees from you and your directions every chance he gets. You could be suffering from infertility, multiple miscarriages, or the heart-wrenching death of a child. Perhaps you're a homeschooling mother who has sacrificed much to keep your children close to your faith and values and to educate them well; yet they're rebelling against everything you do and say, and you're left feeling resentful, hurt, and angry.

There are moms of special-needs children who are undoubtedly special but who also require special grace and love and patience that we mortals can't always readily give. There are single mothers out there just trying to make it through another exhausting, all-consuming, and oftentimes lonely day. I think of my own mother, whose oldest barely spoke to her as a teenager and then fell prey to a drug addiction that left my mother tearful and clutching her rosary beads many a night.

Even the moms who seemingly have it "easy" have to get up day after day, splash cold water on their faces sometimes in lieu of a shower—because, really, who has time for *that*?—and serve, give, and empty themselves over and over, and they're expected to do it all excessively, constantly, and yes, joyfully. That's what Jesus did, right? He could have given far less; one drop of his blood could have saved us all, yet he freely chose to shed every last bit of it. He gave what is beyond "enough" and adequate. If there was more to give, he gave it. Jesus never stopped to count the cost. Nor did he expect something in return. And he didn't even complain about all he had to do, either. Can you imagine if there were a chapter in the New Testament in which Jesus grumbled about dying on the Cross for a bunch of pitiful sinners who didn't appreciate him?

Talk about a lot of pressure. Is it any wonder we try so desperately hard to convince others we are joyful mothers? But we seem to forget that Jesus, in his suffering, also did two other very important things.

First, he admitted he was afraid and in pain. One of the most beautiful and hopeful Bible passages for me is when Jesus yells, "My God, my God, why have you forsaken me?" (Mt 27:46).

Why are we so afraid of doing the same—of admitting our own feelings of fear and abandonment? If I'd stopped trying so hard to bury my feelings of despair and to pretend life was peachy and I was happy when clinical depression took hold of me and just cried out sooner than I did, things would not have been so difficult for so long. You have to want to accept love, grace, and help more than you want to appear like you have it all together.

When we're faced with defiant children, when we're suffering from the blues or full-blown depression, when we feel alone and unsupported in our roles as mothers, when we feel hopeless and like we've ruined our children for life, or when we lose a child to miscarriage, sickness, or an accident, remember this: like Jesus, there will be moments as a mother when you find yourself in a passion. Here you are in a position of powerlessness that you did not choose but in which God asks you to be faithful. He wants your trust more than your control.

Now, some of your "passions" as a mother may seem small in comparison to what others are grappling with, but be careful not to compare crosses. If something is tough for you, then it's tough. My dear friend Cathy Adamkiewicz, author of *Broken and Blessed: A Life Story*, lost her daughter Celeste when she was only four months old. Once I was apologizing to her for complaining about toothpick-like crosses such as sleep deprivation when she had endured so much, but her response surprised me. She said, "People assume that Celeste's death is the biggest cross I've ever had. I'm not so sure that's the case. Sometimes it's the tiny crosses that we must endure repeatedly that are the hardest to pick up and carry."

She went on to explain that despite how terribly difficult it was to lose a child, the redemptive part of the suffering was much more transparent. There were throngs of people supporting, praying, and encouraging her entire family, and she said God's love and presence in her life was palpable. But when we're dealing with those daily toothpick crosses, we can often feel so much more alone and like God is distant.

So whatever your cross is and however small you may think it is, don't deny it. Pick it up. Embrace it. But don't think that you're pathetically weak just because it's heavy and it hurts you.

Believe there will be pain in motherhood and in life. Accepting suffering is the first step in giving it redemptive power. You don't have to apologize for bleeding. Jesus didn't. God doesn't ask that of you, and neither should anyone else.

WE ALL NEED OUR SIMONS AND VERONICAS

The second beautifully humble act Jesus did that we too often skim over is he accepted help. Jesus fell physically. As a mother, you're going to fall, too. But when you do, that's when the Simon of Cyrenes and Veronicas will step forward to help you. And it's our job to accept their help. It's also our job to reach out to others with compassion, not judgment, when they are suffering. I know a very strong Christian woman whom I admire. She knows theology inside and out and can fluently quote scripture, but she's not the best at being compassionate. Once in her presence, I started to cry. My snuffling embarrassed me, but I took a deep breath and shared about some of my brokenness. She shifted in her seat and quickly tried to change the subject, and I could tell my vulnerability made her feel uncomfortable. On the other hand, my husband's default response to seeing my struggle is almost always an "I can fix this" attitude. But sometimes we're not looking to be fixed. We just need help carrying our loads.

We can't get through life all on our own. We weren't designed that way. We were created to need God as well as the help of others to get through tough days, cancer diagnoses, financial troubles, parenting challenges, mental health disorders, or whatever trials life has in store for us. What we need from each other more than judgment is compassion. Compassion doesn't necessarily mean you'll understand what someone is going through; it just means you'll love them in spite of it and be there for them. My own mom, despite having had many crosses to bear in her life, is naturally programmed to be happy. She doesn't always "get" depression or people who worry excessively. But she also doesn't judge them or think that she's any better than them. She listens, she prays, and she loves.

Like it or not, as mothers we're in the trenches. And just like soldiers, we need people who've got our backs and are going to give us cover. Sometimes during times of peace, we can laugh at our kids' antics and share our favorite parts of being a mom. But there are times when motherhood is more like a war (a battle of wills, a grueling campaign for sleep or pooping on the potty), and we can either be the medic and offer our support to fellow moms or humbly accept help as the wounded soldier.

I was extremely embarrassed when I broke down and cried in front of a circle of women during my serious depression. A few of the women present were merely close acquaintances, and I remember later apologizing and trying to laugh off my breakdown like I wasn't mental or anything. But each of these women provided support and refused to see me as anything but a hurting woman who needed their prayers and love. Two of the women in the room that day have become some of my closest friends. They know about that sad, dark, and scary time, and I'm no longer embarrassed but grateful that they can help me keep healthy and set appropriate boundaries with others who may not be as generous, understanding, or kind with my sickness. These women also see my willingness to be honest and vulnerable as a strength rather than a weakness. Similarly, when

Jesus washed the disciples' feet, it revealed his humility and servanthood. When we open ourselves to the ministry of others and God's graces, we're doing the same.

I love a mother who loves her children and selflessly gives, but I really, really love an authentic mother who accepts that heartache, frustration, and a need for a glass of wine at the end of the day often accompany the joy and laughter even raising the easiest of children brings.

WHEN JOY IS ELUSIVE, SEEK HOPE

Through my own relentless quest to be a perpetually joyful mother and subsequently feeling like a big loser when I've felt anything but warm and fuzzy feelings in the trenches, I have learned that what a Christian mother's heart must hold close to—even more than perennial joy sometimes—is hope.

What exactly is hope? It's not some glittery unicorn desperate moms are chasing.

> Hope is the theological virtue by which we desire the kingdom of heaven and eternal life as our happiness, placing our trust in Christ's promises and relying not on our own strength, but on the help of the grace of the Holy Spirit. "Let us hold fast the confession of our hope without wavering, for he who promised is faithful." . . . The virtue of hope responds to the aspiration to happiness which God has placed in the heart of every man; it takes up the hopes that inspire men's activities and purifies them so as to order them to the Kingdom of heaven; it keeps man from discouragement; it sustains him during times of abandonment; it opens up his heart in expectation of eternal beatitude. (CCC, 1817–1818)

Being a mom isn't always—or ever!—going to be heaven on earth, but we have the hope that an eternity spent in heaven is what we have to look forward to.

I doubt Jesus was joyful when the nails were being driven into his hands. I doubt Mary's heart was singing a happy ditty as she watched her innocent, amazing son suffer and die. But both of them were hopeful.

Joseph of Arimathea took the body of Jesus down from the Cross, and sweet Mary received him into her arms. Mary had lost her son and was left only with faith in God's eternal promise. When all seems lost, when in our arms we hold our deep sorrow, we must turn our eyes to Mary, the most blessed of believers, and trust that we do not suffer in vain.

Motherhood—and just being a human being in this broken world—requires a hopeful heart. It requires the hope that there is light at the end of the darkness, that there *is* a point to all this—if simply to love the best we know how and to trust that God's grace will fill in the cavernous gaps.

Hope also reminds us of a phrase that's become a regular mantra of mine when I'm facing a particularly rough patch as a parent: *this too shall pass.* Newborn babies grow up and won't always be feeding constantly or in constant need of mama's soothing arms. When I learned that my son's preschool teachers had to remove all the toy kitchen utensils because he was turning them into weapons, I held my feisty, 100 percent testosterone-filled boy close and allowed my heart to whisper, "This too shall pass. His weapons one day will be faith, love, kindness, and given all of his giggles, a sense of humor in the wake of life's disappointments."

Yet a warning, my dear mothers: If you're waiting for something that just feels too big to pass—and I'm not talking about an in utero baby, a stuck kidney stone, or a constipated toddler's bowel movement—if there's something sucking every ounce of happiness out of you despite your "efforts" to make things or yourself better or if you're *really* hurting and unable to climb out of a dark pit, seek help. *Now*. Don't be ashamed. This doesn't mean something is wrong with you or that you're not a super mom. You just may need some help to feel super again.

I recently met a mother who confided in me and shared a story about a day when she threw something across the room, scaring her children. She felt out of control, and having suffered from a major depressive episode in college, she knew it was time to get help. Counseling and cognitive behavioral therapy went a long way in helping her to feel like herself again. "I don't understand why there's such a stigma with getting help for mental health problems," she said. "We outsource help from experts all the time, and there's nothing more important to your family than being a healthy mom inside and out."

I also had a mama friend once admit that she was tired of her "crazy emotions," but she also had tried every "natural" remedy and just couldn't seem to feel like her old self. I reminded this beautiful, strong mother that Jesus—God himself—cried out to his Father and begged, "Take this cup away from me" (Lk 22:42).

Seeking help is *not* a sign of weakness. Sometimes the best thing you can do for your family is to take care of yourself. Others may not understand or may even minimize your suffering. So be it. You're not here to please them.

In the Christian community, having a mental illness can be somewhat of a scarlet letter. After all, we're supposed to have the joy of the resurrected Christ in our hearts. This is the source of our joy, not anything else. Therefore, if we believe in Jesus, how can we ever be sad, anxious, or obsessive-compulsive about something as meaningless as our weight or turning off lights in our homes? Many Christians feel like neither they—nor anyone else—should need "happy pills" or anything aside from their faith to feel content and "normal." It's tempting to think that a person with a stronger faith would be able to handle the tidal waves of sadness and worry. As someone who knows the pain of depression and anxiety all too well, that is rubbish. I was reluctant to take any medications for a long time and sometimes would dangerously and abruptly stop taking a prescription even if it was helping me to feel more balanced. My kind, patient husband has reminded me on more than one occasion that I would never expect my sister-in-law, who has type 1 diabetes, to just pray harder to make her pancreas work. Her body needs insulin to be healthy. Some of our bodies may need certain medications in order to balance brain chemicals or wayward hormones. There's no shame in accepting help—even if it's in the form of a pill.

We all have bad days. Depression, anxiety, and other mental health disorders are not just bad days. Their symptoms last longer than a couple of days and interfere with the ability to function on a daily basis. One in four Americans suffer from some form of mental illness, according to the National Alliance on Mental Illness. No one should suffer hopelessly when there are a variety of successful treatment options available. (Please see appendix A for resources on finding help.)

If no other truth penetrates your heart from this chapter, let this one sink deep: whether you're a born optimist or not; an easygoing mother or more type A; an extrovert, introvert, or somewhere in between; there will be a time or lots of times when you rightfully feel that there is simply nothing left to give. You are depleted and drained. If a crisis arose, you do not know from where you would possibly squeeze out one more ounce of energy. You desperately want to believe God is there and that he is willing and ready to help. You cry out,

> O God, you are my God—
> it is you I seek!
> For you my body yearns;
> for you my soul thirsts,
> In a land parched, lifeless,
> and without water. (Ps 63:2)

Yet your prayers dissipate into the air. But here's what you must do: get up (or ask others to help you if you can't do it on your own), and ready yourself for come what may. Not because you feel strong or feel replenished but because you know (hope!) God is there whether you *feel* him or not. God is present even if your strength is absent. And so you step out in faith—not because you feel he has given you what you need now but because you know he will . . . eventually. It is then you hear him say, "My grace is sufficient for you, for power is made perfect in weakness" (2 Cor 12:9).

Mom's Time-Out

Dear God, I hurt so badly, and I don't know how to make it stop. So today I turn to some of the saints, these intimate friends of Christ, who struggled and were flawed just as I am. St. Julian of Norwich, you believed good came from everything. "All shall be well" was your mantra. Help me to embrace this even when I feel like life is hard and joyless. St. Dymphna, you are the patron of those suffering from nervous and mental afflictions. You know what it means to feel weak. Help me to not focus on all that I lack and what I cannot do on my own but instead to remember all that God can do through me. And dear St. Jude, patron of hopeless causes, you have turned many desperate situations around. Come to my aid now, and remind me that nothing is impossible with God. Amen.

A beautiful book that has helped me to take up my crosses willingly in life, as well as to be open with others about my suffering and trials, is *He Leadeth Me*. The author, Jesuit Fr. Walter J. Ciszek, was captured by Russians during World War II, convicted of being a "Vatican spy," and spent twenty-three years in Soviet prisons and Siberian labor camps. Yet he never stopped clinging to hope.

He writes, "The greatest grace God can give such a man is to send him a trial he cannot bear with his own powers—and then sustain him with his grace so he may endure to the end and be saved."[1] Ask God to help you to see the challenges you face as a parent and your joyless moments as a gift of grace from him. Are there moments in your life when you clearly witnessed the redemptive value of suffering? What did you learn from these times in your life? If you personally are not suffering and find that joy comes easily to you, consider how you might show compassion to someone who is hurting.

Conclusion

FINDING FREEDOM FROM
FEAR IN MOTHERING

Each Advent season, my family heads out to a local Christmas tree farm in search of the perfect tree. I'm honestly okay with a Charlie Brown–tree, but my detail-oriented husband is a perfectionist about things of which I am not and always has a hard time selecting our tree. The kids show him their favorites, and he inevitably finds a bald spot or notices the tree's overall shape is too sparse or too asymmetrical. Eventually, he reluctantly acquiesces with one of the kids' selections after I remind him no real tree is going to be a flawless shape and height. But wouldn't we rather have real than artificial?

Then we return home, and that's when I start wanting things to be perfect. The tree is just a tree, but the memories we make decorating that said tree better be glittery-gold. So I make homemade cocoa. The girls dip candy canes into warm pools of chocolate. Then they watch *How the Grinch Stole Christmas!* as my husband laces the tree with multicolored lights. None of that elegant only-white-light business for the Wicker tree; that's not the kind of perfection I'm after. We do bold and bright in our house.

The same holds true for the ornaments. There are no themes. The decorative danglers cover the gamut from homemade angels with pictures of the kids' heads for faces to a bristly hedgehog that was my husband's as a boy.

I love sifting through the bottomless container of ornaments. So many of them conjure up memories or old loves, such as the golden horse head molded out of clay that reminds me of my beloved palomino, Sunny, or the baby's first Christmas ornament that I received during my first month of motherhood. This is a tradition I savor. My children do, too, and I hope these are the moments they will remember instead of the less golden ones, such as the daily fighting that occurs each morning over whose turn it is to open the drawer of our Advent calendar where four M&Ms (all the same color so as to dissuade yet another fight) were hidden.

I don't always get my perfect memories during Advent or other times. That's life. This past year, we gathered around our new tree, and kids started pulling out several ornaments all at once. Then Thomas broke an ornament. It looked like a ball, so he hurled it across the living room. And, of course, all the girls were as sad as if that were their *favorite ornament of all time.* We comforted Thomas because we thought he was scared from the glass ball shattering at his feet. But shortly thereafter, he snagged another ornament off the tree and chucked it across the room where it promptly shattered into colorful shards.

I remember how I felt standing there in the shadow of our beautiful, sparkling tree. I examined the pieces and knew there was no way to salvage that ornament. At that moment, I felt our memories were the same way—like they'd been broken into so many pieces there was no way I could make them happy and whole again.

Nothing seemed to be turning out the way I had hoped or the way I wanted it to. The Advent memories were not very Norman Rockwell-ish at all. We were a mess. And a very noisy one at that.

So I wonder: Will the children's memory banks see past all that? Will they take ornaments out each Christmas and smile fondly, or will they remember the shards reflecting the tear-stained faces in their broken shininess?

And what if they do? Does that make their life any less meaningful and good? Maybe Advent is supposed to be a little sad because we so desperately need a Savior. Maybe motherhood and childhood aren't always supposed to be magical but real and, yes, tough. Maybe just like our tree, imperfectly real is better than artificial. We are broken, hurting. We're not always satisfied. We need hope—Christ—to be born in our hearts. But we're also not anything like that shattered ornament. We can always be redeemed and pieced back together.

I'd like to think my children will grow up with only happy childhood memories, yet I'm a memory maker, not a memory keeper. My kids might have some glum recollections, but perhaps they will have the Christmas memories, too. The memories where we all got it right—not *perfect* but right for the moment. There were broken ornaments and sometimes broken promises, too. There were silly stories and happily-ever-afters, but there were tearjerkers thrown in there as well, with endings that weren't all neat and tidy. There was a mother who did her best. Sometimes that wasn't nearly good enough for what her children and family deserved. But many times it was. There was hurt, but there was love that was inexorably linked to mercy and forgiveness.

And there was always grace, and it almost always was born out of the darkness. It came in the child who hugged a tired mama. It came in a "just because" note that compared mom to a flower everyone wants to be around that a child scribbled down and shyly handed to me. It came in an apology. Grace filled our hearts as we filled cups each dinnertime—cups that sometimes splattered and spilled and needed to be refilled. Grace slipped into our lives just when we needed it. It was a gift that grabbed hold of hearts even if we were lousy at preparing ourselves for it. Somehow, like Christmas for the Grinch's Whos, it came all the same without packages, boxes, or bags. Without perfect mamas, perfect children, or perfect memories. Grace was there. Joy was there. This is what I hope, God willing, these children of mine might remember.

CARRY ON, CHRISTIAN SOLDIER-MOTHER

I have several childless friends. Outwardly, it might seem that their decision to not have children is because of their careers, desire to travel, or reluctance to not be tied down. Yet I know there's sometimes something deeper keeping them from entering motherhood.

Once, after a few glasses of wine, one of my child-free friends confided in me that the real reason she didn't want to bring children into the world was because she was afraid. She couldn't get past the anxiety of all that might go wrong if she became a mother. She was fearful for the children she might never have. Her fear was not self-seeking; it came from a place of love and a desire to do what she thought was right. My beautiful friend was afraid she would be an awful mother, and as she's great at her career and being a wife, why screw things up?

I know a woman who does have a child and has told me she has pondered having another one, but she just can't make the jump. She makes things happen in the workplace, yet she can't make her child poop on the potty or do much of anything else. In a hushed whisper, she confesses she'd like to have another child, but she's afraid—not just about finances and all that practical stuff—because she feels like her child deserves a better mother. Yes, she knows the joy of being a mom and how it makes her a better person. But sometimes, she fears, it makes her a worse person. Sometimes it hurts so viscerally, she's not sure she can handle any more of it. She loves her child, but she doesn't always love being a mother.

When my first child was put into my arms, I experienced pro-found joy, but I felt terrified, too. I wasn't afraid of dropping my baby on her head or of sudden infant death syndrome, although trimming those tiny nails on those pink, delicate fingers made me twitchy. My husband seemed to worry more about germs and all the potential physical dangers. My fears were more of the emotional variety. Before becoming a mother, people and our society seemed to vocalize the more concrete, potential consequences of having children. I was informed of all that I might lose once that squawking little one was placed in my arms—money, my body, spontaneity, sleep. But even as I did start to lose some of those things, those weren't the kinds of things that kept me up at night. More than being wary of all that I might lose, I was far more afraid of what I might gain. Once I had a baby, I would have a new insight into my humanity and I would be deeply invested in something I would love with all my being, but that love? Well, it might not be enough. Wrapped right along with that sweet bundle of joy was the sometimes crippling fear that I'd be a bad mother, or a mediocre one at best, and that despite caring so much, maybe too much, I'd make a mess not only of my own life but of those lives entrusted to me.

Talking to other moms—not in a conversational, superficial way but when we really get to the heart of things and strip off our happy mommy masks—I know none of us is alone in our fears.

But we're also not alone in our courage to give motherhood a try and to keep on trying every single day.

It's these fears each of us has to overcome every time we say yes to a new life or welcome a child through adoption. It's these fears we slowly find freedom from when we realize that God has our backs and we just have to trust in him, his help, and his grace, which have no price and are ours for the taking. We find further freedom when we free ourselves from our own expectations and when we let go of fear and anxiety enough to let hope in.

G. K. Chesterton said, "If a thing is worth doing, it is worth doing badly."[1] But we don't want to do things badly. Getting fired from a job stinks, but feeling like you nurtured a bad seed or raised a terribly unhappy child? I'm not sure I could handle that. But what if I'd caved in to those fears? What if we all did? Being a parent is worth it—even when you make mistakes. Which we do. All of the time.

Here's the thing about us parents, more specifically us Christian parents: if we believe in God then we believe in hope. We believe in redemption. We believe in light being born out of darkness. We bank on God's compassion when we, in our human weakness, don't dole it out to our children very freely or when we're not compassionate with ourselves. We slip, we stumble, we screw up as parents, but God somehow makes good out of the mess we create or that is created for us and is out of our control. Wrong decisions may take us out of God's will but not out of his reach. We may not always see evidence of the goodness, but we believe it is there. If we don't, then we're not really believers.

As for being imperfect parents to imperfect children, we don't give up on our children or ourselves, but sometimes we do have to give our children and ourselves up to God. Whether we're worried about money, losing our identity, or just being a lousy parent, we turn to him. We trust. Sometimes we may feel as if we're fighting a losing battle, but God never abandons his servants. Sometimes he lets us see the fruit of our work, but sometimes he doesn't.

I wish I could convince my childless friend to take the maternal plunge by telling her that parenthood is the path to pure bliss, but then I'd be lying. Sometimes parenting a child is the path to frustration, heartbreaking sadness, financial woes, health worries, and more. Having a child makes you more vulnerable than ever before. I don't know what the future holds for my own children—the ones who are here with me today and the ones who might end up under my care in the future. I like to think that with five children, luck is on my side and at least one will remember to call and visit when he or she's grown.

If any of my deeply rooted fears become a reality, I know what I must do. I must not play the blame game. I'll have to hold on to hope and detach myself from thinking I can save my child—or from the belief that if I don't save her or keep her from harm or unhappiness, it's because I'm a lousy mother. I may have to let go of the very happiness our world lauds and says we're in control of and should seek.

Most of us who have chosen to have children—or those who have to accept unexpected pregnancies with grace and trust— probably do see children as bringing happiness and adding something meaningful to our lives. Children will grow up to be the adults who will someday save us all, we might tell our childless friends or those who devalue human life at conception. Upon closer scrutiny, however, none of these things may actually end up being true, at least not all of the time. Yet every child we add to our families and our world serves as an ambassador of hope, a reminder that the future is worth investing in and sticking around for.

Having children sometimes brings happiness, but it's when it doesn't that it becomes even more apparent that accepting the call to parenthood is one of the bravest and most hopeful things we can do. Motherhood isn't necessarily a source of fulfillment and complete joy. We don't find our worth in our children or in our maternal aptitude. Our worth lies in our identity as beloved daughters of God. Even if we know and accept these truths and have faith and hope in our Savior, it doesn't mean we will be immune to twinges of inadequacy or feelings of anxiety and dread. But it should mean we don't allow these feelings to get the best of us.

Pope Francis released *Amoris Laetitia*, his document on family, when I was still writing this book. As is his custom, he coupled compassion with ideology. Pope Francis wrote, "We have to realize that all of us are a complex mixture of light and shadows. The other person is much more than the sum of the little things that annoy me. Love does not have to be perfect for us to value it. The other person loves me as best they can, with all their limits, but the fact that love is imperfect does not mean that it is untrue or unreal."[2]

Dear Mamas, imperfect love is still love. Don't hold back because you're afraid you won't offer "perfect" to your children or your family. Good enough is enough, especially when it's paired with God's grace. Put yourself out there, and "do not let your hearts be troubled" (Jn 14:1). You've got this, Mom, even when you think you don't.

afterword

BY LISA M. HENDEY

Over my last twenty-five years of motherhood, I've had many sleepless nights, and on occasion, I've wondered what kept our Blessed Mother up at night. As I rocked a colicky infant, I imagined Mary rocking baby Jesus in a cradle that Joseph had crafted as she stared down at her son's face with wonder. When my preteens' big algebra tests or unfinished college applications had me tossing and turning (even though my own math-impaired abilities were not being examined), I would wonder what role Mary might have played in Jesus' education and studies. And most recently, when being the mom of young adult men has often meant insomnia bouts miles and miles away from where my sons slumber, I find myself reflexively reaching for my rosary and imploring Mary with Ave Marias. She faced this phase, right? Jesus' pulling away toward total independence? Her saying good-bye to the son who once lived in her womb and fed at her breast as he embraced his public ministry? Did Mary ever face the same heartache, regrets, and "what if" moments I find myself pondering these nights?

In this lovely book you hold in your hands, Kate Wicker has penned for us moms a love letter, a hope-filled emancipation from the prison of self-imposed perfectionism that plagues not only young moms but mature ones, too. I wish—since I'm so much older than many of you reading this book—that I could assure you that you'll outgrow the need to please in the same way your baby sons outgrow their car seats or your daughters their favorite sparkly shoes. But I can't. If that phase happens for moms, I haven't gotten there yet.

But I've learned over the years through the wisdom of mentor moms in my own life that what Kate has taught us here is true for each of us in our own matchless ways. Just as God lovingly created you uniquely to be his precious daughter, he lovingly instilled in you exactly those gifts you need to mother in your way. The "mentor moms" I turn to for wisdom—most often unspoken but moreso taught to me in deed rather than word—are many and varied. Some are my elders; two are my own mom and best friend, Anne, who has parented my four siblings and me for a half a century, and my mother-in-law, Norma, who is now teaching me to unfailingly love my future daughter-in-law as she's loved me. Some are my peers, like my dear friends Mara and Martha who have stood beside me since our long-gone days on sandy playdates pushing swings and swapping crazy mom stories. From my younger sisters, who gave me both wisdom and the great joy of being Auntie Lisa, I've learned the art of balancing career and commitment to family.

But some of my greatest mom mentors will likely never know the impact they've had on my life. Our time together might have been fleeting, but the lessons they imparted were intense: a Midwestern single mother who chose life for her son, a grandmother in the Philippines who gathered her grandchildren under the roof of her tiny home while their parents went to the city to earn a living, and the soybean farming moms in Tanzania who took me into the fields they till under a baking sun to scratch out extra income so their children could go to school. You won't find any of these matronly superheroes on Pinterest, but their mark on this world and on my heart is indelible.

Some of my mom mentors are women who began for me as holy card images but have evolved into intercessory prayer companions: St. Monica, who has taught me to pray without ceasing for my sons while at the same time separating their spiritual journeys from my own; St. Zélie Martin, who most surely planted the seeds for a profound little way in her daughter's soul; and St. Elizabeth Ann Seton, whose personal conversion experience made her spiritual mother to so many.

And what about Mary, mother of the Incarnate Word? The lists of questions I would ask her fill my journals. In my moments of imperfection, she is most frequently on the receiving end of my litanies of woe or wonder. Between decades, I whisper my insecurities, tucking them into her Immaculate Heart with confidence that she carries them to the One whose divine will guides my days.

You won't outgrow imperfection, my dear mom friends. But if you are wise enough to implement even a portion of the wisdom Kate Wicker has so generously and humanly shared in these pages, you'll have a great start toward finding the peace, joy, and love you so richly deserve. I urge you to get this book good and dirty from overuse and to share it with others in your life who will become your set of mentor moms. And I invite you to become a part of our virtual family at CatholicMom.com, where you will find sisters in Christ who are anxious to walk this crazy journey alongside you.

Our Lady, Queen of Peace, pray for us!

Acknowledgments

I've often said that words are like babies and come when they're ready. This book was in its embryonic stage for a long time, and it took a whole lot of discernment, grace, patience, prayers, and support from myriad people for it to finally fully develop. A big thanks goes out to Heidi Saxton for encouraging me to keep writing and for helping me to organize my ideas and the stories of my heart. You were one of the first editors I worked with when I started to transition from solely writing for secular journalism to writing for Catholic media, and you've always helped me to be a better writer and to not take my writing or myself so seriously.

Thank you, Lisa Hendey, for believing in this project from day one and for going to bat for me. I am forever grateful for your support, prayers, professional guidance, and friendship.

Behind every good book is an even better editor. Thank you, Kristi McDonald. You were such a pleasure to work with because you get mothering, perfectionism, writing, and *me*. You made my writing so much better.

This book never would have been possible without the steady and generous help of grandparents. Nearly once a week, Nana,

Pop, Gaba, and/or Papa stepped in and took care of my kids so I could write. My children are so lucky to have such a close relationship with all of their grandparents, and I'm blessed to have free, dependable babysitting. You guys are the greatest.

Thanks, too, to my husband. He didn't think I should write this book because he knows full well that I am still very much a perfectionist in recovery and didn't want me to end up with too full of a plate. Yet when I said yes, he did, too. I love you so much, Dave. Our love is as eternal as diaper changes and sleeplessness.

A big shout out to my Clover peeps. What I would I do without you? Aside from drink less wine and laugh not as much. And thanks to all my friends and fellow moms for sharing their hearts and their stories. We're in this together. Let's always build one another up and look out for each other.

Last but never least, thanks be to God. "For from him and through him and for him are all things. To him be glory forever. Amen" (Rom 11:36).

appendix a

ADDITIONAL RESOURCES

1. QUEEN MOMMY

The Catherine of Siena Institute (www.siena.org) has a wonderful website that can help you identify your spiritual gifts.

A friend confided in me that she really doesn't know if she has any special gifts. Nor can she think of anything aside from mothering that makes her feel happy and fulfilled. I've encouraged her to think back to when she was a child and to consider what she enjoyed then, and I encourage you to do the same.

3. PERFECTIONISM, SUPERMOM'S KRYPTONITE

Brené Brown's *The Gifts of Imperfection: Let Go of Who You Think You're Supposed to Be and Embrace Who You Are* ought to be required reading for every perfectionist in recovery. I have had countless people recommend the book to me, and two friends gave it to me as a gift—if that tells you something about me. Brown's website (brenebrown.com) also offers workshops, free downloads, and more, to help you live what she's coined a "wholehearted life."

8. WHEN THERE'S NO JOY
IN MOTHERING OR IN LIFE

Seeking help for a mental health sickness is the first courageous step toward healing. A "stronger" character or faith will not make a mental illness go away. Listed below are a few resources that might offer you help and hope.

- Find a Catholic therapist at www.catholictherapists.com
- Postpartum Support International: www.postpartum.net, 1-800-944-4773
- PPD Moms: Postpartum Depression Resources, www.1800ppd-moms.org, 1-800-PPD-MOMS
- National Suicide Prevention Hotline, 1-800-273-8255
- National Alliance on Mental Illness, www.nami.org

Even after we get help medically, we may still have trouble finding total healing. We all have times when we feel weighed down by our mistakes. You may feel incapable of turning to the Lord, and you may even wonder if God has abandoned you. A wise spiritual director can help guide you closer to God's mercy and forgiveness. We often think that mercy is only a gift we receive once we've already turned back to him or gone to Confession. In reality, it was God's constant mercy that inspired us to return to God in the first place.

SpiritualDirection.com is a wonderful resource that explains spiritual direction, how to find a spiritual director, the spiritual direction process, and more.

appendix B

READING GROUP GUIDE

1. QUEEN MOMMY

1. Read Mark 10:17–30. Why do you think Jesus tells this young man to give away all that he has? Such radical poverty wasn't part of his everyday preaching. Jesus' problem with the young man wasn't his wealth itself: it was the way his wealth controlled him. We all participate in some form of idolatry. It's part of our fallen nature. We make idols out of money, celebrities, sex, fitness, food, recreation, work, and yes, motherhood. Have you ever made being a mother your highest calling? Do you sometimes over-glorify your mothering role? What were (are) some of the negative ramifications of your doing this? Jesus' message to the rich man is really a message to all of us. We can't place any-thing—even good things like being an attentive mom—above our call to love and serve him.

2. How strong is your love for God? List anything you think you're tempted to love more than Jesus. Why is it so difficult to put God first and to love and trust him? Now consider how

intimacy between two people grows. How can you develop a closer relationship with God? Through prayer? Scripture reading? Adoration? Write down at least one spiritual resolution that you'll try to adopt that will help you grow closer to Christ.

3. Aside from your relationship with God, write down any other relationships in your life that need more of your love and attention and perhaps a little work. What can you do this week to nurture these relationships?

4. Write down some of your gifts and talents. If this is difficult for you, ask someone who knows you well and whom you love and trust to tell you the gifts she sees in you. How can you best use these gifts to bring Jesus to others? Remember, sharing with others doesn't have to be extravagant or earn you a big paycheck. I have a friend who is wonderful at opening her home to others. She always makes me feel welcome and really does have an open door policy. I've learned a lot from her and have started to worry less about the way my house looks and learned to focus more inviting others in.

2. I LOVE MOTHERHOOD—EXCEPT WHEN I DON'T

1. Do you sometimes struggle with admitting that motherhood is tough? Why or why not?

2. The scriptures are rich with passages espousing the joy children bring. Passages such as "When she has given birth to a child, she no longer remembers the pain because of her joy that a child has been born into the world" (Jn 16:21) are important for us to pray over, but we also have to remember that Jesus told his disciples, "Suffer the little children to come unto me" (Mt 19:14, KJV). Raising children is tough, and every mother is going to suffer sometimes. You don't achieve holiness overnight, but

you might through your daily "scourges" in mothering. What are some of the toughest challenges you're currently facing as a mother? Remember that what is hard for you may not be hard for your friend and vice versa. Are there any strategies you could take to lessen the burden of these more difficult challenges? Or is this something you simply need to accept with grace and trust? Whatever the case, throughout your day, ask Jesus for his strength, and try to offer up those tough moments—the spills, the broken curfews, the middle-of-the-night puke fests—for the greater glory of God.

3. I often find that motherhood becomes joyless for me when I forget to just have fun with my kids. Most of us are natural care-givers, and we can get so caught up in the caring of our children that we forget to just enjoy them. Try not to turn mothering into a project or just another "thing" to do. What delights you and your children and causes you to lose track of time? How can you incorporate these "joy-givers" more into your weekly, if not daily, routine?

4. Love, especially sacrificial, biblical love, doesn't come easy. Try to choose love only for the moment rather than telling yourself you will love with patience and kindness always and forever as a mother. Whenever you're having a hard time feeling love or even expressing it for your children or for your vocation of motherhood, pray an Act of Love:

> O my God, I love you above all things, with my whole heart and soul, because you are all good and worthy of all my love. I love my neighbor as myself for the love of you. I forgive all who have injured me and I ask pardon of all whom I have injured. Amen.

3. PERFECTIONISM, SUPERMOM'S KRYPTONITE

1. In what area(s) of your life do you struggle with perfection? Do you long for a perfect home or body or for perfectly behaved children? Try to identify the fear behind your striving for perfection. For example, when I was suffering from an eating disorder, my unhealthy habits transcended my desire to look a certain way. What I was really afraid of was being unlovable and not being in control. Nowadays, when I foolishly try to control my kids' behavior and make them appear "perfect," especially out in public, what I'm really worried about is that others will see their imperfect actions and either assume I'm a bad mother or they're bad children. Letting go of my own imperfection has demanded that I replace my fear with trust. Perfectionism is often rooted in pride, an overconfidence in self, and its antidote is having more faith and confidence in God. In what areas of your life do you need to hand over the reins to God?

2. Has there been a past situation in your life in which you relinquished your control and fear and gave your trust completely to God—and then the unexpected happened? If yes, share what you learned from the experience.

3. Remember, every saint is a sinner who tried day after day to give his or her best. If anyone is in Christ, he is a new creation. Old becomes new (see 2 Cor 5:17). God is the author of new beginnings. Some of us make "perfect" our bar because we are haunted by our sins and are afraid that if we make one misstep, we'll be headed down the path of wretchedness. However, past sins can't define us—or our kids. Is there a past sin—either your own or one your child may have committed—that has wounded you deeply, so much so that you're having a tough time letting go of it? What can you do to help yourself make peace with the past and find joy in the present?

4. Overcoming perfectionism doesn't mean we settle for mediocrity. We can always pray for strength to strive for excellence. What personal disciplines do you struggle with in your own life? How can you take baby steps toward strengthening these weaknesses? I personally struggle with patience and have to pray for Christ's strength on a daily basis, take a deep breath, and not let my emotions get the best of me. I also have to work on forgiving myself when I lose it and just start over instead of letting one lapse snowball into an awful day.

5. Is there someone in your life to whom you can acknowledge and expose your needs, fears, and imperfections? Why is it often easier to hide behind a veneer of "I'm fine" than to be vulnerable?

6. Are you more of a people-pleaser than a God-pleaser? How does your worry about what others may think of you influence your actions? What concerns you the most: the need to be authentic or the need to be liked and accepted? Why?

4. LET THE MOTHERING GAMES BEGIN!

1. Why do you think mothers fall into the comparison trap so frequently? How has the role of social media contributed to increased feelings of inadequacy in mothers? Has jealousy of another mom—in real life or on the Internet—ever obscured your perception of God's will for your own life? Explain.

2. Have you ever been guilty of neglecting your own gifts and strengths as a mom simply because you know someone else who is more gifted than you are? Are you "hiding your talents"? How does God feel about that (read Mt 25:14–30)?

3. What are some ways you might be able to minister to fellow mothers, especially those you have a hard time being around because of feelings of jealousy or inadequacy? Could you make

a meal for a mother who has her hands full? What about volunteering to watch another mom's children so she can get a little break? How can you make it a habit to be deliberate in showing kindness to your fellow mothers?

4. Make a list of mothers who have influenced you—for better or worse. Now ask yourself if you hold anything against anyone on this list. How can you work toward forgiveness? On the contrary, is there someone on the list whom you find yourself idolizing? Have you allowed your respect for this person to result in you putting yourself down? What would be a better response? How can you replace your adoration, which belongs to God only, for this person with simple admiration? What have you learned from each person on this list?

5. Humility, I used to feel, was thinking less of myself, when really, it is rooted in thinking more of others. Women with humble hearts are not tempted to compare or compete. They are rooted in love and acceptance rather than fear or insecurity.

The Litany of Humility is a beautiful prayer that helps us keep our pride and vanity in check.

> O Jesus! meek and humble of heart, Hear me.
> From the desire of being esteemed,
> Deliver me, Jesus.
>
> From the desire of being loved . . .
> From the desire of being extolled . . .
> From the desire of being honored . . .
> From the desire of being praised . . .
> From the desire of being preferred to others . . .
> From the desire of being consulted . . .
> From the desire of being approved . . .
> From the fear of being humiliated . . .
> From the fear of being despised . . .
> From the fear of suffering rebukes . . .

From the fear of being calumniated . . .
From the fear of being forgotten . . .
From the fear of being ridiculed . . .
From the fear of being wronged . . .
From the fear of being suspected . . .

That others may be loved more than I,
Jesus, grant me the grace to desire it.

That others may be esteemed more than I . . .
That, in the opinion of the world,
others may increase and I may decrease . . .
That others may be chosen and I set aside . . .
That others may be praised and I unnoticed . . .
That others may be preferred to me in everything . . .
That others may become holier than I,
provided that I may become as holy as I should . . .

5. MOM THE MARTYR

1. How does God's view of a servant contrast with the world's view of a servant? Which definition of servant are you more closely fulfilling right now? Why?

2. Are you having a difficult time discerning the difference between biblical sacrificial love and what our society might define as being a loving, giving mother? Pray over Matthew 11:28–30: "Come to me, all you who labor and are burdened, and I will give you rest. Take my yoke upon you and learn from me, for I am meek and humble of heart; and you will find rest for yourselves. For my yoke is easy, and my burden light." Do you think following Christ guarantees mothering will be easy? Why? Do you think God's yoke is lighter than the cultural pressures we unnecessarily burden ourselves with?

3. Be careful to not equate love with meeting every single need of your children. We cannot push ourselves as if we are limitless. Even Jesus didn't heal every disease or meet every need he encountered, and he's God. Write down a list of things you feel you must do for your family. Now reread the list. What are your motives behind each area of service? What was Jesus' motive (see Jn 6:38)? Cross off any items on your list that are not backed by authentic, godly motives.

4. Self-care is critically important for moms. It might feel like you have absolutely no time to give to yourself, but if you're running on empty, it's going to be difficult to give to your children or enjoy their company. Even Jesus knew he could not exclusively serve others while neglecting his own physical and spiritual needs. He frequently withdrew from crowds, and he took time to rest. What is your biggest obstacle to carving out some alone time? Brainstorm together on how you each can overcome some of these obstacles.

5. Do you struggle with asking for help? Why? Do you fall into the martyr mom trap because you're convinced that no one could care for your children or do some specific mothering task as well as you can? How can you relinquish control and invite others to help in the lives of you and your children?

6. Jesus had to balance the expectations of his family with God's plan for him, just like you do. Read Luke 2:41–52. Mary and Joseph expected Jesus to stay close by, yet they lost him in the temple. After they were reunited, Jesus obediently went home with them; however, he made it clear that being in his Father's house—and being obedient to God—was a priority. Are you held prisoner to your family's expectations—so much so that your obedience to God is lacking? How can you shift your priorities and help your family to have more realistic expectations of you and what you can offer them as their mother?

6. I AM MOTHER! HEAR ME ROAR!

1. Prayerfully read Acts 9:1–9. Invite God to make known areas in your life that you're seeking to control rather than "letting go and letting God," and write them down.

2. Describe your biggest parenting fears. Now look at those fears through the eyes of an all-powerful, loving God. How do they look under his watch?

3. In talking to moms while writing this book, I discovered a common fear in many Christian mothers is that their children will abandon the beliefs in the God we hold so dear. I have an aunt who has five beautiful daughters, and all but one have abandoned their faith. "Somewhere, we dropped the baton of faith, she says. "I don't know when or how. All of my girls are good, and I know God is merciful, but it makes me sad." True conversion is the Holy Spirit's business, not our own. Servant of God Elisabeth Leseur was a devout Catholic married to an atheist. She kept a secret diary and often reflected upon how she felt called to focus on her own soul rather than converting her husband's. She writes, "Let [my husband Felix] see the fruit but not the sap, my life but not the faith that transforms it, the light that is in me but not a word of him who brings it to my soul; let him see God without hearing his name. Only on those lines, I think, must I hope for the conversion and sanctity of the dear companion of my life, my beloved Felix."[1] After Elisabeth's death, Felix discovered her journal and later not only converted to the faith but also became a priest. She died not with answers but with faith. What are some ways you can share your faith without words and endless sermonizing?

4. The Serenity Prayer is an oldie but a goodie and one of my favorite prayers to pray when I'm faced with a parenting challenge I can't control or may not even understand. Consider

praying it daily, especially if you find yourself struggling with
relinquishing control.

> God, grant me the serenity
> to accept the things I cannot change,
> Courage to change the things I can,
> and the wisdom to know the difference.
> Living one day at a time;
> Enjoying one moment at a time;
> Accepting hardship as the pathway to peace.
> Taking, as he did, this sinful world as it is,
> not as I would have it.
> Trusting that he will make all things right
> if I surrender to his will;
> that I may be reasonably happy in this life,
> and supremely happy with him forever in the next.
> Amen.

7. THE OLD WOMAN WHO LIVED IN A SHOE

1. What season of motherhood has been the most challenging
for you? Why?

2. Do you struggle with the physical and/or emotional aspects
of aging? Why or why not?

3. Has your plan for your family turned out the way you always
hoped? Why or why not? Has the superiority of God's plan been
revealed to you yet? If not, how can you better trust in him and
patiently wait for his goodness to be revealed?

4. Read Ecclesiastes 3:17. Are you trying to do something in your
current season of motherhood that God would prefer you to wait
to embrace in a later season?

5. No matter what season of life you find yourself in, keeping Christ at the center of your life will ensure you have the graces to tackle what comes your way and will also help you find joy in the moment. Have you boxed God into just another thing on your to-do list? Or does his love for you spill over onto everything you encounter on any given day? How can you invite Jesus into every moment of your day and be more aware of his presence?

6. Do you struggle with living in the present? Why or why not? Is it harder for you to let go of the past or to look too far ahead for the future? Read about the Holy Spirit in the following scripture passages: Ephesians 3:14–19; Romans 8:14; Acts 9:31; and John 14:16. How might the Holy Spirit help you to live more joyfully in the present, to seek the grace of the moment, and to face the challenges of the whatever season you find yourself in right now?

8. WHEN THERE'S NO JOY IN MOTHERING OR IN LIFE

1. Maybe you're naturally a more easygoing or optimistic mom who doesn't struggle with finding joy in mothering or in life, and instead you find it difficult to empathize with someone who grapples with depression or hardship. Are you stingy with sharing grace? Why? Does suffering make you feel uncomfortable? Do you know someone going through a hard time? Ask God to help reveal how you might best minister to this person, and pray for a compassionate heart.

2. Do you know of a mom who could use some encouragement? Write her a letter today telling her what a great mom she is and why.

3. Once my preschooler asked me to write down a prayer she was making up. This is all she said to me: "Is God here? Yes. Yes, he is." I wrote down her words with shaky hands because

her "prayer" could not have come at a more appropriate time. I was dealing with postpartum depression and in many ways, I felt abandoned. Spiritual dryness along with the hormone-induced depression I was experiencing had made God seem aloof to me—like a really happy and good idea but not someone who desired intimacy with me. Yet my preschooler's simple, childlike faith reminded me that God is with me even when I'm the one who's shutting him out. God's not likely to show up as flash of lightning or a saintly vision to most of us, but he's always there, most often in the seemingly small details, corners, and childlike prayers of our lives. Do you sometimes have trouble recognizing God's love for you or even believing in him? How can you be more open to God's presence in your life? How can you cooperate with God so that he can turn your struggles, suffering, and spiritual dryness into a blessing?

4. Read 1 Timothy 6:11–16. Is there an area of your life where you're tempted to give into despair rather than fighting "the good fight"? How can you better handle your discouragement? Don't be afraid to seek help. An "I can fix it" attitude only goes so far; we were created to need God and one another. There is no shame in admitting your struggles and inviting others to help lessen your burdens.

5. Would you describe yourself as a hopeful person? Why or why not? How would you define hope? Now consider how the Church defines it:

> Hope is the theological virtue by which we desire the kingdom of heaven and eternal life as our happiness, placing our trust in Christ's promises and relying not on our own strength, but on the help of the grace of the Holy Spirit. "Let us hold fast the confession of our hope without wavering, for he who promised is faithful." . . . The virtue of hope responds to the aspiration to happiness which God has placed in the heart

> of every man; it takes up the hopes that inspire men's
> activities and purifies them so as to order them to the
> Kingdom of heaven; it keeps man from discourage-
> ment; it sustains him during times of abandonment; it
> opens up his heart in expectation of eternal beatitude.
> Buoyed up by hope, he is preserved from selfishness
> and led to the happiness that flows from charity. (CCC
> 1817–1818)

Hope isn't just a glittery unicorn we may find ourselves desperately chasing. It's a real virtue born from Jesus' resurrection and
one we can cultivate throughout our lives. If you're struggling
with finding hope in a certain situation, read John 16 and medi-
tate on the following passages: "Your grief will become joy" (Jn
16:20), and "In the world you will have trouble, but take courage,
I have conquered the world" (Jn 16:33).

6. One of the most well-known passages of St. Teresa of Avila's
writings is the prayer of trust. All mothers—from the ones who
suffer with clinical depression to the moms who have a hard
time relinquishing control—ought to hold this prayer near to
their hearts.

> Let nothing trouble you, let nothing frighten you,
> All things pass away, but God never changes.
> Patience obtains all things, for she who possesses God
> Wants for nothing . . . God alone suffices.

notes

INTRODUCTION: FEAR IN MOTHERING

1. Raymond Arroyo, ed., *Mother Angelica's Little Book of Life Lessons and Everyday Spirituality* (New York: Doubleday, 2007), 171.

2. Brené Brown, *The Gifts of Imperfection: Let Go of Who You Think You're Supposed to Be and Embrace Who You Are* (Center City, MN: Hazelden, 2010), 82.

1. QUEEN MOMMY

1. John Paul II, *Letter to Women*, June 29, 1995, no. 2, www.vatican.va.

2. Józef Mindszenty, *The Mother*, quoted in Emily Cavins, Patti Armstrong, Jeff Cavins, and Matthew Pinto, *Amazing Grace for Mothers: 101 Stories of Faith, Hope, Inspiration, and Humor* (West Chester, PA, Ascension Press, 2004), 19.

3. Francis de Sales, as quoted in Carol Kelly-Gangi, ed., *The Essential Wisdom of Saints* (New York: Fall River, 2008), 17.

4. I wrote *Weightless: Making Peace With Your Body* (Cincinnati: Servant Books, 2011) for any woman who has struggled with her relationship with her body, food, or weight. As someone who battled a clinical eating disorder and is all too familiar with body image angst, I desire to give hope to women to reclaim the beauty of creation and to know that their beauty runs much deeper than a number on the scale.

2. I LOVE MOTHERHOOD—EXCEPT WHEN I DON'T

1. Anne Tyler, *Ladder of Years* (New York: Ballantine, 1995), 24.

3. PERFECTIONISM, SUPERMOM'S KRYPTONITE

1. Brown, *The Gifts of Imperfection*, 56–57.
2. Jacques Philippe, *Interior Freedom*, trans. Helena Scott (New York: Scepter, 2007), 33.
3. Ibid., 37.
4. Teresa of Avila, *The Interior Castle: Study Edition*, trans. Kieran Kavanagh, O.C.D. and Otilio Rodriguez, O.C.D. (Washington, DC: ICS Publications, 2010), 145.

4. LET THE MOTHERING GAMES BEGIN!

1. Thérèse of Lisieux, *Story of a Soul: The Autobiography of Saint Thérèse of Lisieux*, trans. John Beevers, 2nd ed. (New York: Doubleday, 1976), 2; emphasis added.
2. Thérèse of Lisieux, as quoted in Gretchen Rubin, *The Happiness Project: Or, Why I Spent a Year Trying to Sing in the Morning, Clean My Closets, Fight Right, Read Aristotle, and Generally Have More Fun* (New York: HarperCollins, 2009) e-book.
3. Meg Meeker, *The 10 Habits of Happy Mothers: Reclaiming Our Passion, Purpose, and Sanity* (New York: Ballantine, 2011), e-book.

5. MOM THE MARTYR

1. Caryll Houselander, "Giving Ourselves Unreservedly to Life," in *Wood of the Cradle, Wood of the Cross*, quoted in Karen Lynn Krugh, "Seeing Christ in All People," Catholic Culture, accessed February 2, 2016. https://www.catholicculture.org/culture/library/view.cfm?recnum=528.
2. Benedict XVI, *Letter of His Holiness Benedict XVI to the Faithful of the Diocese and City of Rome on the Urgent Task of Educating Young People*, January 21, 2008, www.vatican.va.
3. Lisa M. Hendey, *A Book of Saints for Catholic Moms: 52 Companions for Your Heart, Mind, Body, and Soul* (Notre Dame, IN: Ave Maria Press, 2011), 109.
4. Ibid., 129.

6. I AM MOTHER! HEAR ME ROAR!

1. Joseph Esper, *Saintly Solutions to Life's Common Problems* (Manchester, NH: Sophia Institute Press, 2001), 206–207.

7. THE OLD WOMAN WHO LIVED IN A SHOE

1. Faisal Hoque, "To Exist Is to Change," Huffington Post, accessed May 30, 2016. http://www.huffingtonpost.com/faisal-hoque/to-exist-is-to-change_b_4910337.html.
2. Philippe, *Interior Freedom*, 47.
3. Tal Ben-Shahar, *Happier: Learn the Secrets to Daily Joy and Lasting Fulfillment* (New York: McGraw-Hill Education, 2007), e-book.
4. Joyce Rupp, *God's Enduring Presence: Strength for the Spiritual Journey* (New London, CT: Twenty-Third Publications, 2008), 113.

8. WHEN THERE'S NO JOY IN MOTHERING OR IN LIFE

1. Walter J. Ciszek, *He Leadeth Me* (San Francisco: Ignatius Press, 1995 reprint), 71.

CONCLUSION: FINDING
FREEDOM FROM FEAR IN MOTHERING

1. G. K. Chesterton, *What's Wrong with the World* (Amazon Digital Services, 2012), e-book.
2. Francis, *Amoris Laetitia* (*The Joy of Love*), April 8, 2016, no. 113.

APPENDIX B: READING GROUP GUIDE

1. Elisabeth Leseur, *The Secret Diary of Elisabeth Leseur: The Woman Whose Goodness Changed Her Husband from Atheist to Priest* (Manchester, NH: Sophia Institute Press, 2002), 70.

KATE WICKER is an author, speaker, health columnist for *Catholic Digest*, and regular contributor to Relevant Radio's *Morning Air* program. Her work also has appeared in *Woman's Day*, *Pregnancy*, *Family Fun*, WhatToExpect.com, *Atlanta Parent*, *Faith & Family LIVE!*, *Crisis*, FathersforGood.org, Catholic News Agency, *Catholic Exchange*, and *CatholicMom.com*.

Wicker earned a bachelor's degree in journalism from the University of Georgia (summa cum laude) in 2000. She is the author of *Weightless: Making Peace with Your Body* and has contributed to *The Handbook for Catholic Moms* and *Word by Word*. Wicker also was featured on the *Momnipotent* DVD. She and her husband, Dave, have five children. They live in Athens, Georgia.

AVE
AVE MARIA PRESS

Founded in 1865, Ave Maria Press,
a ministry of the Congregation of
Holy Cross, is a Catholic publishing
company that serves the spiritual and
formative needs of the Church and its
schools, institutions, and ministers;
Christian individuals and families; and
others seeking spiritual nourishment.

For a complete listing of titles from

Ave Maria Press

Sorin Books

Forest of Peace

Christian Classics

visit www.avemariapress.com

AVE MARIA PRESS
AVE | Notre Dame, IN
A Ministry of the United States Province of Holy Cross